The Super Easy Air Fryer Cookbook

2000 Days of Delectable and Health-Conscious Recipes to Uplift Your Cooking Skills

Deborah J. Ward

Copyright© 2023 By Deborah J. Ward Rights Reserved

This book is copyright protected. It is only for personal use. You cannot amend, distribute, sell, use, quote or paraphrase any part of the content within this book, without the consent of the author or publisher.

Under no circumstances will any blame or legal responsibility be held against the publisher, or author, for any damages, reparation, or monetary loss due to the information contained within this book, either directly or indirectly.

Disclaimer Notice:

Please note the information contained within this document is for educational and entertainment purposes only. All effort has been executed to present accurate, up to date, reliable, complete information. No warranties of any kind are declared or implied. Readers acknowledge that the author is not engaged in the rendering of legal, financial, medical or professional advice. The content within this book has been derived from various sources. Please consult a licensed professional before attempting any techniques outlined in this book.

By reading this document, the reader agrees that under no circumstances is the author responsible for any losses, direct or indirect, that are incurred as a result of the use of the information contained within this document, including, but not limited to, errors, omissions, or inaccuracies.

Editor: AALIYAH LYONS

Cover Art: DANIELLE REES

Interior Design: BROOKE WHITE

Food stylist: Sienna Adams

Table Of Contents

Introduction	1	Crispy Crackling Bites	12
		Bacon BBQ	12
Chapter 1		Mexican Muffins	13
Appetizers	8	Coconut Cheese Sticks	13
Air Fryer Ham Tarts	9	Delicata Squash	13
Corn Tortilla Chips	9	Garlic Roasted Mushrooms	13
Roasted Bell Pepper	9		
Roasted Spicy Hot Dogs	10	**Chapter 2**	
Spinach Quesadilla	10	**Breakfasts**	14
Pizza Bites	10	Cinnamon Pancake	15
Honey Roasted Carrots	10	French Frittata	15
Brussels Sprouts With Feta Cheese	10	Breakfast Cheese Bread Cups	15
Bacon Avocado Wraps	11	Deviled Eggs With Pickle Relish	16
Spinach Frittata	11	Almond Milk Bake	16
Eggplant Fries	11	Eggs With Peppers	16
Curried Brussels Sprouts	11	Garlic Zucchini Spread	17
Parmigiana Tomato Chips	12	Eggs Ramekins	17
Brussels Sprout Crisps	12	Broccoli Casserole	17

Tomato Omelet	18	Smoked Paprika Chicken	31
Air Fried Vegan Breakfast Bread	18	Chicken Fillet	32
Breakfast Chicken Strips	18	Pepper Turkey Bacon	32
Prosciutto and Spinach Egg Cups	19		
Grilled Cheese Sandwiches	19	**Chapter 4**	
Rolls With Bacon And Cheese	19	Beef, Pork and Lamb	33
Green Scramble	20	Air Fry Rib-Eye Steak	34
Bacon Cups	20	Basil Pork	34
Scrambled Eggs	20	Air Fryer Hamburgers	34
Breakfast Mini Cheeseburger Sliders	21	French-Style Smothered Pork Chops	34
Paprika Cauliflower Bake	21	Onion Beef Bites	35
Dill Omelet	21	Bacon With Shallot And Greens	35
Cinnamon And Cheese Pancake	22	Mustard Pork	35
Hash Browns	22	Air Fryer Pork Taquitos	35
Eggplant Spread	23	Tomato Rib Eye Steaks	36
Peanut Butter And Banana Breakfast Sandwich	23	Fried Pork Chops	36
		Lamb Chops With Herb Butter	36
Air Fryer Bacon	23	Garlic Pork Chops	36
		Hot Dogs	36
Chapter 3		Pork Bondiola Chop	37
Poultry	24	Parmesan Beef Meatballs	37
Air Fryer Brown Rice Chicken Fried	25	Beef Empanadas	37
Rolled Turkey Breast	25	Vinegar Pork Chops	37
Chicken Thighs Smothered Style	25	Crunchy Canadian Bacon	38
Cinnamon Chicken Thighs	25	Beef & Mushrooms	38
Tangy Chicken With Parsley And Lime	26	Classic Keto Cheeseburgers	38
Chicken Sausage In Dijon Sauce	26	Ginger Lamb	38
Paprika Duck	26	Coconut Beef Steak	39
Pesto Chicken	27	Jamaican Pork With Jerk	39
Almond Meatballs	27	Thyme and Turmeric Pork	39
Mozzarella Turkey Rolls	27	Smoked Pork	39
Wine Marinated Turkey Wings	27	Taco Pork	40
Taco Chicken	28	Cheesy Pork Chops In Air Fryer	40
Ginger Drumsticks	28	Pork Rind	40
Coriander Chicken Drumsticks	28		
Teriyaki Hen Drumsticks	28	**Chapter 5**	
Faire-Worthy Turkey Legs	29	Fish & Seafood	41
Turkey Breast	29	Asian Sesame Cod	42
Bacon-Wrapped Turkey With Cheese	29	Breaded Hake With Green Chili Pepper	42
Almond Coconut Chicken Tenders	30	Air Fryer Salmon Cakes	42
Easy Blackened Chicken	30	Air Fried Cajun Salmon	42
Sweet Chicken Wings	31	Tuna Melt	43
Nutmeg Chicken Fillets	31	Restaurant-Style Flounder Cutlets	43
Tomato Chicken Mix	31	Oregano Fish Sticks	44

Bacon Scallops	44
Miso Fish	44
Crunchy Red Fish	44
Breaded Fish	45
Crumbed Fish	45
Lime-Garlic Shrimp Kebabs	45
Air Fried Salmon Cakes	46
Rosemary Shrimp Skewers	46
Sesame Seeds Coated Tuna	46
Parmesan Walnut Salmon	47
Onion Shrimps	47
Sweet Tilapia Fillets	47
Salmon With Honey Glaze	48
Air-Fried Cajun Shrimp	48
Nacho-Crusted Shrimp	48
Air Fried Catfish	49
Salmon With Maple Soy Glaze	49
Air-Fried Crumbed Fish	50
Blackened Salmon	50
Air Fryer Salmon With Maple Soy Glaze	50

Chapter 6
Side Dishes and Snacks — 51

Mini Pizza	52
Mozzarella Snack	52
Cheesy Bell Pepper Eggs	52
Potato Chips	52
Coriander Fennel	53
Broccoli Hash Brown	53
Cabbage Steaks	53
Broccoli Tots	53
Turmeric Cauliflower Rice	54
Air Fryer Squash	54
Eggplant Mash	54
Spicy Green Beans	54
Pumpkin Skinny Chips	55
Turmeric Tempeh	55
Keto Coleslaw	55
Rutabaga Bites	55
Vegetable Roast	56
Radishes	56
Baked Bell Peppers Salad	56
Kidney Bean Popcorn	56

Acorn Squash Slices	57
Air Fryer Sweet Potato	57
Air Fryer Avocado Fries	57

Chapter 7
Vegan & Vegetarian — 58

Elegant Garlic Mushroom	59
Cheesy Kale	59
Nutmeg Okra	59
Kid-Friendly Zucchini Fries	60
Paprika Asparagus	60
Vegetable Salsa Wraps	60
Sriracha Golden Cauliflower	61
Paprika Kale and Olives	61
Crispy Black-Eyed Peas	61
Caribbean Fried Peppers With Tofu	62
Spicy Celery Sticks	62
Lemony Green Beans	62
Balsamic Garlic Kale	63
Zucchini Balls	63
Tangy Asparagus And Broccoli	63
Sesame Fennel	64
Potato with Creamy Cheese	64
Crispy Brussels Sprout Chips	64
Coconut Mushrooms Mix	64
Chili Lime Broccoli	65
Garden Fresh Green Beans	65

Chapter 8
Desserts — 66

Blackberry Cream	67
Deep Fried Snickers	67
Cocoa Spread	67
Keto Butter Balls	68
Baked Molten Lava Cake	68
Almond Cookies	69
Pineapple Sticks with Yogurt Dip	69
Spiced Apples	69
Italian Cheese Chips	70
Cream Cups	70
Almond Bars	70
Lemon Berry Jam	71
Peanut Cookies	71

Chocolate Bacon Bites	71	Appendix 1 Measurement Conversion Chart	74
Apple Hand Pies	71		
Berry Cookies	72	Appendix 2 The Dirty Dozen and Clean Fifteen	75
Chocolate Hazelnut Turnovers	72		
Midnight Nutella Banana Sandwich	73	Appendix 3 Index	76
Cinnamon Sugar Dessert Fries	73		
Apple Dumplings	73		

Introduction

Welcome to "The Super Easy Air Fryer Cookbook"! If you're holding this book in your hands, it's a safe bet that you're either an air fryer aficionado or someone eager to dive into the exciting world of air frying. Either way, you're in for a culinary adventure that will tantalize your taste buds and simplify your cooking routines.

Air frying has taken the culinary world by storm, and for good reason. It's a revolutionary method of cooking that offers a healthier alternative to traditional frying, with results that are nothing short of extraordinary. In this cookbook, we aim to demystify the art of air frying, introduce you to its principles, and equip you with the knowledge and recipes to make the most of this remarkable kitchen appliance.

The Basics of Air Frying

So, what exactly is air frying, and how does it work? Air frying is a cooking technique that uses hot air circulation to cook food. Unlike deep frying, which immerses food in oil, air frying relies on a powerful fan and a heating element to create a crisp and delicious outer layer while keeping the interior moist and tender. It's essentially a mini convection oven that fits right on your countertop.

One of the key principles of air frying is the rapid movement of hot air. This constant circulation of air cooks your food evenly and quickly, resulting in that signature crispy texture without the excessive use of oil. The ability to achieve a similar level of crispiness with significantly less oil is one of the major advantages of air frying. It's a game-changer for anyone who enjoys the crunch and flavor of fried food but wants to cut back on unhealthy fats.

The Benefits of Air Fryers

Air fryers offer a multitude of benefits that make them a kitchen essential:

Healthier Eating

Let's start with the most compelling advantage: healthier eating. By using little to no oil, air frying reduces the fat content of your favorite fried foods while retaining their delicious taste and texture. Say goodbye to greasy, calorie-laden meals, and hello to a healthier lifestyle.

Time-Saving

Air fryers are exceptionally efficient at cooking food. They preheat quickly and cook faster than traditional ovens. Whether you're making a quick weekday dinner or a weekend feast, your air fryer can cut down on cooking time, leaving you with more time to savor your meals.

Versatility

Air fryers are incredibly versatile. They can roast, bake, grill, and even dehydrate. The range of recipes you can create with an air fryer is practically endless. From crispy French fries and juicy chicken wings to delectable desserts, your air fryer can do it all.

Easy Cleanup

No one enjoys scrubbing pots and pans after a meal. Air fryers typically come with non-stick baskets or trays that are a breeze to clean. With minimal oil splatter and no deep frying mess, *cleaning up after air frying is a simple task.*

Energy Efficiency

Air fryers are more energy-efficient than conventional ovens. They require less energy to heat up and maintain a consistent cooking temperature, saving you money on your utility bills.

Compact Design

The compact size of air fryers makes them perfect for kitchens of all sizes. They won't take up much counter space, making them an ideal addition to any kitchen.

How to Use Your Air Fryer

- Using an air fryer is incredibly straightforward, but there are a few tips and tricks to ensure you get the best results:
- Preheat Your Air Fryer: Just like your oven, it's a good idea to preheat your air fryer before cooking. This ensures that your food cooks evenly and crisps up nicely.
- Don't Overcrowd the Basket: To achieve that desired crispy texture, avoid overcrowding the air fryer basket. Give your food some space to allow for proper air circulation.
- Oil Wisely: While you can use a minimal amount of oil for some recipes, you can also invest in an oil spray bottle to distribute a thin, even layer of oil on your food. This will help achieve the crispy finish you're looking for.
- Check and Shake: Midway through the cooking time, it's a good idea to check and shake your food for even cooking. This is especially important for foods like french fries or chicken wings.
- Experiment: Don't be afraid to experiment with your air fryer. Try new recipes, tweak cooking times, and discover what works best for your taste buds. Air frying is all about getting creative in the kitchen.

Using This Cookbook

Now that you're equipped with the basics of air frying, let's talk about how to use this cookbook. "The Super Easy Air Fryer Cookbook" is designed to make your culinary journey as smooth and enjoyable as possible. Here's a quick guide to help you navigate through the recipes and get the most out of this book:

Recipe Format

Each recipe in this book follows a simple and easy-to-follow format. You'll find a list of ingredients, clear instructions, and helpful tips for every dish. We've done our best to make sure that every recipe is approachable, whether you're a seasoned chef or just starting your cooking adventure.

Recipe Categories

This cookbook is divided into different categories to help you find exactly what you're craving. From appetizers and snacks to main courses and desserts, you'll discover a wide range of recipes to satisfy your taste buds.

Getting Creative

Feel free to get creative with these recipes. Once you've mastered the basics, you can experiment with different seasonings, ingredients, and cooking times to create your own unique dishes.

Let's Get Started

Whether you're a seasoned air fryer pro or just starting to explore this fantastic cooking method, "The Super Easy Air Fryer Cookbook" has something for everyone. From classic comfort foods to innovative, healthy dishes, you'll find a wide range of recipes to tantalize your taste buds and simplify your cooking routine.

We're excited to take this culinary journey with you and introduce you to the world of air frying. So, what are you waiting for? Let's get started and uncover the magic of air frying together. Get ready to enjoy delicious, crispy, and guilt-free meals in no time. Happy air frying!

Air Fryer Cooking Chart

Beef					
Item	Temp (°F)	Time (mins)	Item	Temp (°F)	Time (mins)
Beef Eye Round Roast (4 lbs.)	400 °F	45 to 55	Meatballs (1-inch)	370 °F	7
Burger Patty (4 oz.)	370 °F	16 to 20	Meatballs (3-inch)	380 °F	10
Filet Mignon (8 oz.)	400 °F	18	Ribeye, bone-in (1-inch, 8 oz)	400 °F	10 to 15
Flank Steak (1.5 lbs.)	400 °F	12	Sirloin steaks (1-inch, 12 oz)	400 °F	9 to 14
Flank Steak (2 lbs.)	400 °F	20 to 28			

Chicken					
Item	Temp (°F)	Time (mins)	Item	Temp (°F)	Time (mins)
Breasts, bone in (1 1/4 lb.)	370 °F	25	Legs, bone-in lb.)	380 °F	30
Breasts, boneless (4 oz)	380 °F	12	Thighs, boneless (1 1/2 lb.)	380 °F	18 to 20
Drumsticks (2 1/2 lb.)	370 °F	20	Wings (2 lb.)	400 °F	12
Game Hen (halved 2 lb.)	390 °F	20	Whole Chicken	360 °F	75
Thighs, bone-in (2 lb.)	380 °F	22	Tenders	360 °F	8 to 10

The Super Easy Air Fryer Cookbook

Pork & Lamb						
Item	Temp (°F)	Time (mins)	Item	Temp (°F)	Time (mins)
Bacon (regular)	400 °F	5 to 7	Pork Tenderloin	370 °F	15
Bacon (thick cut)	400 °F	6 to 10	Sausages	380 °F	15
Pork Loin (2 lb.)	360 °F	55	Lamb Loin Chops (1-inch thick)	400 °F	8 to 12
Pork Chops, bone in (1-inch, 6.5 oz)	400 °F	12	Rack of Lamb (1.5 - lb.)	380 °F	22
Flank Steak (2 lbs.)	400 °F	20 to 28			

Fish & Seafood						
Item	Temp (°F)	Time (mins)	Item	Temp (°F)	Time (mins)
Calamari (8 oz)	400 °F	4	Tuna Steak	400 °F	7 to 10
Fish Fillet (1-inch, 8 oz)	400 °F	10	Scallops	400 °F	5 to 7
Salmon, fillet (6 oz)	380 °F	12	Shrimp	400 °F	5
Swordfish steak	400 °F	10	Sirloin steaks (1-inch, 12 oz)	400 °F	9 to 14
Flank Steak (2 lbs.)	400 °F	20 to 28			

Vegetables					
INGREDIENT	**AMOUNT**	**PREPARATION**	**OIL**	**TEMP**	**COOK TIME**
Asparagus	2 bunches	Cut in half, trim stems	2 Tbsp	420°F	12-15 mins
Beets	1 1/2 lbs	Peel, cut in 1/2-inch cubes	1 Tbsp	390°F	28-30 mins
Bell peppers (for roasting)	4 peppers	Cut in quarters, remove seeds	1 Tbsp	400°F	15-20 mins
Broccoli	1 large head	Cut in 1-2-inch florets	1 Tbsp	400°F	15-20 mins
Brussels sprouts	1 lb	Cut in half, remove stems	1 Tbsp	425°F	15-20 mins
Carrots	1 lb	Peel, cut in 1/4-inch rounds	1 Tbsp	425°F	10-15 mins
Cauliflower	1 head	Cut in 1-2-inch florets	2 Tbsp	400°F	20-22 mins
Corn on the cob	7 ears	Whole ears, remove husks	1 Tbps	400°F	14-17 mins
Green beans	1 bag (12 oz)	Trim	1 Tbps	420°F	18-20 mins
Kale (for chips)	4 OZ	Tear into pieces, remove stems	None	325°F	5-8 mins
Mushrooms	16 OZ	Rinse, slice thinly	1 Tbps	390°F	25-30 mins
Potatoes, russet	1 1/2 lbs	Cut in 1-inch wedges	1 Tbps	390°F	25-30 mins
Potatoes, russet	1 lb	Hand-cut fries, soak 30 mins in cold water, then pat dry	1/2 -3 Tbps	400°F	25-28 mins
Potatoes, sweet	1 lb	Hand-cut fries, soak 30 mins in cold water, then pat dry	1 Tbps	400°F	25-28 mins
Zucchini	1 lb	Cut in eighths lengthwise, then cut in half	1 Tbps	400°F	15-20 mins

6 | *The Super Easy Air Fryer Cookbook*

Chapter 1

Appetizers

Air Fryer Ham Tarts

Prep time: 5 minutes | Cook time: 20 minutes | Serves 4

- Chopped fresh chives: one tbsp.
- Frozen puff pastry: one sheet, thawed
- 4 large eggse
- 4 tbsp. cooked ham, chopped
- 4 tbsp. of Cheddar cheese, shredded

1. Let the air fryer preheat to 400 °F. Lay puff pastry on a surface and slice into four squares.
2. Add two squares of puff pastry in the air fryer and cook for 8 minutes.
3. Take out from the air fryer and make an indentation in the dough's center. Add one tbsp. Of ham and one tbsp. of Cheddar cheese in every hole. Add one egg to it. Add on the other two squares of pastry. Seal the dough seams with water and pinch.
4. Return the basket to the air fryer. Let it cook for about six minutes.
5. Take out from the basket of the air fryer and cool for 5 minutes.
6. Top with chives and serve hot.

Corn Tortilla Chips

Prep time: 5 minutes | Cook time: 8 minutes | Serves 4

- 4 (6-inch) corn tortillas
- 1 tbsp. canola oil
- 1/4 tsp. kosher salt

1. Stack the corn tortillas, cut them in half, then slice them into thirds.
2. Spray the air fryer basket with non-stick cooking spray, brush the tortillas with canola oil and place them in the basket. Air fry at 360°F for 5 minutes.
3. Pause the fryer to shake the basket, then air fry for 3 more minutes or until golden brown and crispy.
4. Remove the chips from the fryer and place them on a plate lined with a paper towel. Sprinkle with the kosher salt on top before serving warm.

Roasted Bell Pepper

Prep time: 10 minutes | Cook time:20 minutes |Serves 4

- 1 teaspoon olive oil
- 1/2 teaspoon thyme
- 4 cloves garlic, minced
- 4 bell peppers, cut into fourths

1. Start by putting your peppers in your basket and drizzling them with olive oil. Make sure they're coated well and then roast for fifteen minutes.
2. Sprinkle with thyme and garlic, roasting for an additional three to five minutes. They should be tender and serve warm.

Roasted Spicy Hot Dogs

Prep time: 10 minutes | Cook time: 20 minutes | Serves 6

- 6 hot dogs
- 1 tablespoon mustard
- 6 tablespoons ketchup, no sugar added

1. Place the hot dogs in the lightly greased Air Fryer basket.
2. Bake at 380 degrees F for 15 minutes, turning them over halfway through the cooking time to promote even cooking.
3. Serve on cocktail sticks with the mustard and ketchup. Enjoy!

Spinach Quesadilla

Prep time: 10 minutes | Cook time: 3 minutes | Serves 2

- 2 keto tortillas
- ¼ cup Cheddar cheese, shredded
- ½ cup spinach, chopped
- 1 teaspoon avocado oil

1. Brush the air fryer basket with avocado oil.
2. Then mix Cheddar cheese with spinach and put over the keto tortillas. Fold the tortillas and put in the air fryer basket.
3. Cook them at 400F for 3 minutes.

Pizza Bites

Prep time: 15 minutes |Cook time: 3 minutes |Serves10

- 10 mozzarella cheese slices
- 10 pepperoni slices

1. Preheat the air fryer to 400F. Line the air fryer pan with baking paper and put Mozzarella in it in one layer.
2. After this, place the pan in the air fryer basket and cook the cheese for 3 minutes or until it is melted.
3. After this, remove the cheese from the air fryer and cool it to room temperature.
4. Then remove the melted cheese from the baking paper and put the pepperoni slices on it. Fold the cheese in the shape of turnovers.

Honey Roasted Carrots

Prep time: 10 minutes | Cook time:12 minutes |Serves 4

- 1 tablespoon honey, raw
- 3 cups baby carrots
- 1 tablespoon olive oil
- sea salt & black pepper to taste

1. Put all ingredients into a bowl. Mix well.
2. Prepare your air fryer to 390 F.
3. Cook for 12 minutes.
4. Serve warm.

Brussels Sprouts With Feta Cheese

Prep time: 10 minutes | Cook time: 20 minutes | Serves 4

- 3/4 pound Brussels sprouts, trimmed and cut off the ends
- 1 teaspoon kosher salt
- Non-stick cooking spray
- 1 cup feta cheese, cubed

1. Firstly, peel the Brussels sprouts using a small paring knife. Toss the leaves with salt and lemon zest; spritz them with a cooking spray, coating all sides.
2. Bake at 380 degrees for 8 minutes; shake the cooking basket halfway through the cooking time and cook for 7 more minutes.
3. Make sure to work in batches so everything can cook evenly. Taste and adjust the seasonings. Serve with feta cheese. Bon appétit!

Bacon Avocado Wraps

Prep time: 5 minutes | Cook time: 15 minutes | Serves 4

- 2 avocados, peeled, pitted and cut into 12 wedges
- 12 bacon strips
- 1 tablespoon ghee, melted

1. Wrap each avocado wedge in a bacon strip, brush them with the ghee, put them in your air fryer's basket and cook at 360 degrees F for 15 minutes.
2. Serve as an appetizer.

Spinach Frittata

Prep time: 5 minutes | Cook time: 10 minutes | Serves 4

- 1/3 cup of packed spinach
- 1 small chopped red onion
- 3 eggs
- Salt, pepper
- Shredded mozzarella cheese

1. Let the air fryer preheat to 180 C.
2. Get a skillet and place over a medium flame. Add oil, onion, cook until translucent, add spinach and sauté until half cooked.
3. Beat eggs and season with kosher salt and pepper—mix spinach mixture in it.
4. Cook in the air fryer for 8 minutes or until cooked.
5. Slice and Serve hot.

Eggplant Fries

Prep time: 7 minutes | Cook time: 12 minutes | Serves 3

- 2 eggplants
- ¼ cup olive oil
- ¼ cup almond flour
- ½ cup water

1. Preheat your air fryer to 390°F. Cut the eggplants into ½-inch slices. In a mixing bowl, mix the water, flour, olive oil, and eggplants.
2. Coat the eggplants and add them to the air fryer and cook for 12 minutes. Serve with yogurt or tomato sauce.

Curried Brussels Sprouts

Prep time: 10 minutes | Cook time: 20 minutes | Serves 4

- 1 lb. brussel sprouts, end trimmed & halved
- 2 teaspoons olive oil
- 1 tablespoon lemon juice, fresh
- 3 teaspoons curry powder, divided

1. Start by getting gout in a large bowl and mix your olive oil with a teaspoon of curry powder.
2. Toss your Brussel sprouts in, mixing until well coated. Place them in your air fryer basket, roasting for twelve minutes.
3. During this cooking time, you'll need to shake your basket once.
4. Sprinkle with the remaining curry powder and lemon juice, shaking your basket again.
5. Roast for an additional three to five minutes.
6. Your Brussel sprouts should be crisp and browned. Serve warm.

Parmigiana Tomato Chips

Prep time: 10 minutes | Cook time: 15 minutes | Serves 4

- 4 Roma tomatoes, sliced
- 2 tablespoons olive oil
- Sea salt and white pepper, to taste
- 1 teaspoon Italian seasoning mix
- 1/2 cup Parmesan cheese, grated

1. Start by preheating your Air Fryer to 350 degrees F. Generously grease the Air Fryer basket with nonstick cooking oil.
2. Toss the sliced tomatoes with the remaining ingredients. Transfer them to the cooking basket without overlapping.
3. Cook in the preheated Air Fryer for 5 minutes. Shake the cooking basket and cook an additional 5 minutes. Work in batches.
4. Serve with Mediterranean aioli for dipping, if desired. Bon appétit!

Brussels Sprout Crisps

Prep time: 10 minutes | Cook time: 20 minutes | Serves 4

- 1 pound Brussels sprouts, ends and yellow leaves removed and halved lengthwise
- Salt and black pepper, to taste
- 1 tablespoon toasted sesame oil
- 1 teaspoon fennel seeds
- Chopped fresh parsley, for garnish

1. Place the Brussels sprouts, salt, pepper, sesame oil, and fennel seeds in a resealable plastic bag. Seal the bag and shake to coat.
2. Air-fry at 380 degrees F for 15 minutes or until tender. Make sure to flip them over halfway through the cooking time.
3. Serve sprinkled with fresh parsley. Bon appétit!

Crispy Crackling Bites

Prep time: 10 minutes | Cook time: 50 minutes | Serves 10

- 1 pound pork rind raw, scored by the butcher
- 1 tablespoon sea salt
- 2 tablespoons smoked paprika

1. Sprinkle and rub salt on the skin side of the pork rind. Allow it to sit for 30 minutes.
2. Roast at 380 degrees F for 8 minutes; turn them over and cook for a further 8 minutes or until blistered.
3. Sprinkle the smoked paprika all over the pork crackling and serve. Bon appétit!

Bacon BBQ

Prep time: 2 minutes | Cook time: 8 minutes | Serves 2

- 13g dark brown sugar
- 5g chili powder
- 1g ground cumin
- 1g cayenne pepper
- 4 slices of bacon, cut in half

1. Mix seasonings until well combined.
2. Dip the bacon in the dressing until it is completely covered. Leave aside.
3. Preheat the air fryer, set it to 350°F.
4. Place the bacon in the preheated air fryer. Select Bacon and press Start/Pause.

12 | The Super Easy Air Fryer Cookbook

Mexican Muffins

Prep time: 10 minutes |Cook time: 15 minutes |Serves4

- 1 cup ground beef
- 1 teaspoon taco seasonings
- 2 oz mexican blend cheese, shredded
- 1 teaspoon keto tomato sauce
- cooking spray

1. Preheat the air fryer to 375F. Meanwhile, in the mixing bowl mix up ground beef and taco seasonings. Spray the muffin molds with cooking spray.
2. Then transfer the ground beef mixture in the muffin molds and top them with cheese and tomato sauce.
3. Transfer the muffin molds in the preheated air fryer and cook them for 15 minutes.

Coconut Cheese Sticks

Prep time: 10 minutes |Cook time: 4 minutes |Serves4

- 1 egg, beaten
- 4 tablespoons coconut flakes
- 1 teaspoon ground paprika
- 6 oz provolone cheese
- cooking spray

1. Cut the cheese into sticks. Then dip every cheese stick in the beaten egg.
2. After this, mix up coconut flakes and ground paprika. Coat the cheese sticks in the coconut mixture. Preheat the air fryer to 400F.
3. Put the cheese sticks in the air fryer and spray them with cooking spray. Cook the meal for 2 minutes from each side. Cool them well before serving.

Delicata Squash

Prep time: 5 minutes | Cook time:10 minutes |Serves 2

- 1/2 tablespoon olive oil
- 1 delicata squash
- 1/2 teaspoon salt
- 1/2 teaspoon rosemary

1. Chop the squash in slices of 1/4 thickness. Discard the seeds.
2. In a bowl, add olive oil, salt, rosemary with squash slices. Mix well.
3. Cook the squash for ten minutes at 400 F. flip the squash halfway through.
4. Make sure it is cooked completely.
5. Serve hot.

Garlic Roasted Mushrooms

Prep time: 3 minutes | Cook time: 22 minutes | Serves 4

- 16 garlic cloves, peeled
- 2 tsp. olive oil, divided
- 16 button mushrooms
- 1/2 tsp. marjoram, dried
- 1/8 tsp. freshly ground black pepper
- 1 tbsp. white wine or low-sodium vegetable broth

1. In a baking pan, mix the garlic with 1 tsp. of olive oil. Roast in the air fryer at 350°F for 12 minutes. Add the mushrooms, marjoram, and pepper; stir to coat.
2. Drizzle with the remaining 1 tsp. of olive oil and white wine. Return to the air fryer and roast for 10 minutes more, or until the mushrooms and garlic cloves are tender. Serve.

The Super Easy Air Fryer Cookbook

Chapter 2

Breakfasts

Cinnamon Pancake

Prep time: 15 minutes | Cook time: 16 minutes | Serves 4

- 2 eggs
- 2 cups cream cheese, reduced-fat
- ½ tsp. cinnamon
- 1 pack Stevia

1. Preheat Air Fryer to 330°F.
2. Combine cream cheese, cinnamon, eggs, and stevia in a blender. Pour ¼ of the mixture in the air fryer basket.
3. Cook for 2 minutes on each side. Repeat the process with the rest of the mixture. Serve.

French Frittata

Prep time: 10 minutes |Cook time: 18 minutes |Serves 3

- 3 eggs
- 1 tablespoon heavy cream
- 1 teaspoon herbs de provence
- 1 teaspoon almond butter, softened
- 2 oz provolone cheese, grated

1. Crack the eggs in the bowl and add heavy cream. Whisk the liquid with the help of the hand whisker.
2. Then add herbs de Provence and grated cheese. Stir the egg liquid gently.
3. Preheat the air fryer to 365F. Then grease the air fryer basket with almond butter.
4. Pour the egg liquid in the air fryer basket and cook it for 18 minutes.
5. When the frittata is cooked, cool it to the room temperature and then cut into servings.

Breakfast Cheese Bread Cups

Prep time: 10 minutes | Cook time: 15 minutes | Serves 2

- 2 eggs
- 2 tbsp. Cheddar cheese, grated
- Salt and pepper, to taste
- 1 ham slice, cut into 2 pieces
- 4 bread slices, flatten with a rolling pin

1. Spray the inside of 2 ramekins with cooking spray.
2. Place 2 flat pieces of bread into each ramekin. Add the ham slice pieces into each ramekin.
3. Crack an egg in each ramekin, then sprinkle with cheese. Season with salt and pepper.
4. Place the ramekins into the air fryer at 300°F for 15 minutes. Serve warm.

Deviled Eggs With Pickle Relish

Prep time: 10 minutes | Cook time: 20 minutes | Serves 3

- 5 eggs
- 2 tablespoons mayonnaise
- 2 tablespoons pickle relish
- Sea salt, to taste
- 1/2 teaspoon mixed peppercorns, crushed

1. Place the wire rack in the Air Fryer basket; lower the eggs onto the wire rack.
2. Cook at 270 degrees F for 15 minutes.
3. Transfer them to an ice-cold water bath to stop the cooking. Peel the eggs under cold running water; slice them into halves.
4. Mash the egg yolks with the mayo, sweet pickle relish, and salt; spoon yolk mixture into egg whites. Arrange on a nice serving platter and garnish with the mixed peppercorns. Bon appétit!

Almond Milk Bake

Prep time: 5 minutes | Cook time: 25 minutes | Serves 4

- 2 cups cauliflower, roughly chopped
- 2 ounces Monterey Jack cheese, shredded
- 4 eggs, beaten
- 1 cup organic almond milk
- 1 teaspoon dried oregano

1. In the mixing bowl, mix dried oregano with almond milk and eggs.
2. Pour the liquid in the air fryer basket and add cauliflower and cheese.
3. Close the lid and cook the meal at 350F for 25 minutes.

Eggs With Peppers

Prep time: 5 minutes | Cook time: 20 minutes | Serves 4

- 2 bell peppers, sliced
- 4 eggs, beaten
- 1 teaspoon avocado oil
- ½ teaspoon white pepper

1. Brush the air fryer basket with avocado oil.
2. Then mix the bell peppers with white pepper and put inside the air fryer basket.
3. Pour the beaten eggs over the bell peppers and bake the meal at 360F for 20 minutes.

The Super Easy Air Fryer Cookbook

Garlic Zucchini Spread

Prep time: 10 minutes | Cook time: 15 minutes | Serves 4

- 4 zucchinis, roughly chopped
- 1 teaspoon garlic powder
- 1 tablespoon avocado oil
- ½ teaspoon salt

1. Mix zucchini with garlic powder, avocado oil, and salt.
2. Put the mixture in the air fryer and bake at 375F for 15 minutes.
3. Then blend the cooked zucchini until you get smooth spread.

Eggs Ramekins

Prep time: 5 minutes |Cook time: 6 minutes |Serves 5

- 5 eggs
- 1 teaspoon coconut oil, melted
- ¼ teaspoon ground black pepper

1. Brush the ramekins with coconut oil and crack the eggs inside.
2. Then sprinkle the eggs with ground black pepper and transfer in the air fryer.
3. Cook the baked eggs for 6 minutes at 355F.

Broccoli Casserole

Prep time: 10 minutes | Cook time: 20 minutes | Serves 4

- 2 cups broccoli, chopped
- 4 eggs, beaten
- 1 teaspoon chili flakes
- ½ cup Cheddar cheese, shredded
- 1 teaspoon avocado oil

1. Brush the air fryer basket with avocado oil from inside.
2. Then mix broccoli, eggs, chili flakes, and cheese in the mixing bowl.
3. Pour the liquid in the air fryer and cook the casserole at 370F for 20 minutes.

Tomato Omelet

Prep time: 5 minutes | Cook time: 20 minutes | Serves 4

- 6 eggs, beaten
- 1 tomato, chopped
- 1 teaspoon coconut oil, melted
- ½ teaspoon dried dill
- ½ teaspoon salt

1. Mix eggs with dried dill and salt.
2. Grease the air fryer basket with coconut oil and pour the egg mixture inside.
3. Add chopped tomatoes and cook the omelet for 20 minutes at 365F.

Air Fried Vegan Breakfast Bread

Prep time: 10 minutes | Cook time: 10 minutes | Serves 2

- 1 vegan bread loaf, large
- 2 teaspoons chives
- 2 tablespoons nutritional yeast
- 2 tablespoons garlic puree
- 2 tablespoons olive oil
- salt and pepper to taste

1. Preheat your air fryer to 375°Fahrenheit. Slice the bread loaf (not all the way through). In a bowl, combine the garlic puree, olive oil, and nutritional yeast.
2. Add this mixture on top of the bread loaf. Sprinkle loaf with chives and season with salt and pepper.
3. Place loaf inside of your air fryer and cook for 10-minutes.

Breakfast Chicken Strips

Prep time: 10 minutes | Cook time: 12 minutes | Serves 4

- 1 teaspoon paprika
- 1 tablespoon cream
- 1 lb. chicken fillet
- ½ teaspoon salt
- ½ teaspoon black pepper

1. Cut the chicken fillet into strips. Sprinkle the chicken fillets with salt and pepper. Preheat the air fryer to 365°Fahrenheit.
2. Place the butter in the air basket tray and add the chicken strips. Cook the chicken strips for 6-minutes. Turn the chicken strips to the other side and cook them for an additional 5-minutes. After strips are cooked, sprinkle them with cream and paprika, then transfer them to serving plates. Serve warm.

18 | *The Super Easy Air Fryer Cookbook*

Prosciutto and Spinach Egg Cups

Prep time: 7 minutes | Cook time: 10 minutes | Serves 6

- ½ cup baby spinach
- 6 slices of prosciutto
- ¼ teaspoons of salt and pepper
- 6 eggs

1. Set the temperature of the air fryer to 375°F (190°C). Spray or drizzle the muffin tin with oil, then lay one piece of prosciutto inside each cup.
2. Gently press about 4-5 spinach leaves into the bottom of each cup.
3. Crack and add eggs into cups, one egg for each cup, and sprinkle with a little pepper; they're ready to go into the air fryer.
4. Carefully transfer your muffin tin or muffin cups to the air fryer (do not fill up completely), close, and cook for 10 minutes.

Grilled Cheese Sandwiches

Prep time: 2 minutes | Cook time: 7 minutes | Serves 2

- 4 slices American cheese
- 4 slices sandwich bread
- Pat Butter

1. Warm your air fryer to 360°F. Fill the center of 2 bread slices with two slices of American cheese.
2. Binge an even layer of butter on each side of the sandwich and position it in the hamper of your air fryer in a single layer. Insert toothpicks on the corners of each sandwich to seal.
3. Air-fries the sandwiches for 4 minutes, flipping once, and cook for another 3 minutes until toasted.

Rolls With Bacon And Cheese

Prep time: 8 to 10 minutes | Cook time: 10 minutes | Serves 4

- 1 pound shredded cheddar cheese
- 1 pound rashers bacon
- 8 oz. Pillsbury Crescent Dough

1. Preheat the air fryer to 330°F.
2. Cut the bacon rashers into 1/4-inch strips and combine them with the cheddar cheese. Place aside. Cut the dough sheet into 1-inch-by-1.5-inch pieces.
3. Place an equal quantity of the bacon and cheese mixture in the middle of each dough piece, and then squeeze the corners together to contain the filling.
4. Place the packages in the Air Fryer basket and bake at 330°F for 7 minutes.
5. Bake for 3 minutes more after increasing the temperature to 390°F. Serve hot.

The Super Easy Air Fryer Cookbook | 19

Green Scramble

Prep time: 5 minutes |Cook time: 20 minutes |Serves 4

- 1 tablespoon olive oil
- ½ teaspoon smoked paprika
- 12 eggs, whisked
- 3 cups baby spinach
- salt and black pepper to the taste

1. In a bowl, mix all the ingredients except the oil and whisk them well.
2. Heat up your air fryer at 360 degrees F, add the oil, heat it up, add the eggs and spinach mix, cover, cook for 20 minutes, divide between plates and serve.

Bacon Cups

Prep time: 10 minutes | Cook time: 10 minutes | Serves 3

- 3 eggs
- ½ teaspoon ground paprika
- 3 bacon slices
- 1 teaspoon avocado oil
- 1 teaspoon chives, chopped

1. Brush the ramekins with avocado oil.
2. Arrange the bacon slices in every ramekin in the shape of the circle and bake at 370F for 7 minutes.
3. After this, crack the eggs in the center of every ramekin and bake the meal at 365F for 3 minutes more.
4. Sprinkle the cooked eggs with chives and ground paprika.

Scrambled Eggs

Prep time: 5 minutes | Cook time: 5 minutes | Serves 2

- 4 large eggs.
- ½ cup shredded sharp Cheddar cheese.
- 2 tbsp. unsalted butter; melted.

1. Crack eggs into a 2-cup round baking dish and whisk. Place dish into the air fryer basket.
2. Set the temperature to 400 Degrees F and set the timer for 10 minutes.
3. After 5 minutes, stir the eggs and add the butter and cheese. Let cook for 3 minutes and stir again.
4. Allow eggs to finish cooking an additional 2 minutes or remove if they are to your desired liking.
5. Use a fork to fluff. Serve warm.

20 | *The Super Easy Air Fryer Cookbook*

Breakfast Mini Cheeseburger Sliders

Prep time: 10 minutes | Cook time: 10 minutes | Serves 6

- 1 pound beef ground
- Cheddar cheese, 6 oz.
- 6 dinner rolls
- To taste, season with salt and black pepper.

1. Pre-heat your air fryer to 390 degrees Fahrenheit. Season 6 beef patties with salt and black pepper.
2. Cook the burger patties for 10 minutes in the frying basket.
3. Remove the burger patties from the air fryer, cover them with cheese, and return them to the air fryer for another minute of cooking.
4. Remove the burgers and place them on dinner rolls to serve them warm.

Paprika Cauliflower Bake

Prep time: 5 minutes |Cook time: 20 minutes |Serves 4

- 2 cups cauliflower florets, separated
- 4 eggs, whisked
- 1 teaspoon sweet paprika
- 2 tablespoons butter, melted
- a pinch of salt and black pepper

1. Heat up your air fryer at 320 degrees F, grease with the butter, add cauliflower florets on the bottom, then add eggs whisked with paprika, salt and pepper, toss and cook for 20 minutes.
2. Divide between plates and serve for breakfast.

Dill Omelet

Prep time: 10 minute | Cook time: 15 minutes | Serves 4

- 8 eggs, beaten
- 1 tablespoon dill, dried
- ¼ cup of coconut milk
- ½ teaspoon coconut oil, melted

1. Mix eggs with dill and coconut milk.
2. Brush the air fryer basket with coconut oil and pour the egg mixture inside.
3. Cook the omelet for 15 minutes at 385F.

Cinnamon And Cheese Pancake

Prep time: 5–7 minutes | Cook time: 16 minutes | Serves 4

- 2 eggs
- 2 cups cream cheese, reduced-fat
- ½ tsp. cinnamon
- 1 pack Stevia

1. Preheat Air Fryer to 330°F.
2. Pour ¼ of the mixture in the air fryer basket. Cook for 2 minutes on each side. Repeat the process with the rest of the mix. Serve.

Hash Browns

Prep time: 5 minutes | Cook time: 8 minutes | Serves 4

- 4 potatoes (medium sized)
- ¼ tablespoon freshly ground black pepper
- 1 tablespoon oil
- ½ teaspoon salt

1. To make hash browns, shred the potatoes in a food processor. Put them into a colander and place them under cold water for 1 minute. Drain the colander for a few minutes.
2. Transfer the shredded potatoes to a em out completely for the crispiest hash browns.
3. Add oil and seasonings to the bowl; mix well before adding to the basket of air fryer set at 380°F for 15 minutes. Flip the basket over and repeat on the other side until desired crispness is reached (it should take another 5-10 minutes).

Eggplant Spread

Prep time: 5 minutes |Cook time: 20 minutes |Serves 4

- 3 eggplants
- salt and black pepper to the taste
- 2 tablespoons chives, chopped
- 2 tablespoons olive oil
- 2 teaspoons sweet paprika

1. Put the eggplants in your air fryer's basket and cook them for 20 minutes at 380 degrees F.
2. Peel the eggplants, put them in a blender, add the rest of the ingredients, pulse well, divide into bowls and serve for breakfast.

Peanut Butter And Banana Breakfast Sandwich

Prep time: 10 minutes | Cook time: 6 minutes | Serves 1

- 2 slices whole-wheat bread
- 1 tsp. sugar-free maple syrup
- 1 sliced banana
- 2 tbsp. peanut butter

1. Evenly coat both sides of the slices of bread with peanut butter.
2. Add the sliced banana and drizzle with some sugar-free maple syrup.
3. Heat in the air fryer to 330°F for 6 minutes. Serve warm.

Air Fryer Bacon

Prep time: 2 minutes | Cook time: 10 minutes | Serves 5

- 5 slices (thick-cut) bacon

1. Lay the bacon slices into your air fryer basket, at least 1 inch apart, to cook. Heat the air fryer at 390°F. Cook bacon for 10 minutes until crispy.
2. Drain on a kitchen napkin before serving.

The Super Easy Air Fryer Cookbook

Chapter 3

Poultry

Air Fryer Brown Rice Chicken Fried

Prep time: 10 minutes | Cook time: 10 minutes | Serves 2

- olive oil cooking spray
- 1 cup chicken breast, diced & cooked
- 1/4 cup chopped white onion
- 1/4 cup chopped celery
- 4 cups cooked brown rice
- 1/4 cup chopped carrots

1. Place foil on the air fryer basket, make sure to leave room for air to flow, roll up on the sides.
2. Spray with olive oil. Mix all ingredients and add them on the top of the foil, in the air fryer basket.
3. Give an olive oil spray on the mixture. Cook for five minutes at 390°F.
4. Open the air fryer and give a toss to the mixture. Cook for five more minutes at 390F.

Rolled Turkey Breast

Prep time: 5 minutes | Cook time: 10 minutes | Serves 4

- 1 box cherry tomatoes
- ¼ lb. turkey blanket

1. Wrap the turkey and blanket in the tomatoes, close with the help of toothpicks.
2. Take to Air Fryer for 10 minutes at 390°F.
3. You can increase the filling with ricotta and other preferred light ingredients.

Chicken Thighs Smothered Style

Prep time: 30 minutes | Cook time: 30 minutes | Serves 4

- 8-ounce of chicken thighs
- 1 tsp paprika
- 1 pinch salt
- ½ cup mushrooms
- onions, roughly sliced

1. Let the air fryer preheat to 400°F.
2. Season chicken thighs with paprika, salt, and pepper on both sides.
3. Place the thighs in the air fryer and cook for 20 minutes.
4. Meanwhile, sauté the mushroom and onion.
5. Take out the thighs from the air fryer serve with sautéed mushrooms and onions.

Cinnamon Chicken Thighs

Prep time: 5 minutes |Cook time: 30 minutes |Serves 4

- 2 pounds chicken thighs
- a pinch of salt and black pepper
- 2 tablespoons olive oil
- ½ teaspoon cinnamon, ground

1. Season the chicken thighs with salt and pepper, and rub with the rest of the ingredients.
2. Put the chicken thighs in air fryer's basket, cook at 360 degrees F for 15 minutes on each side, divide between plates and serve.

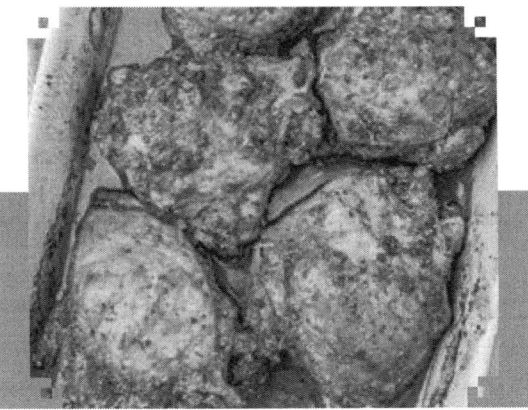

Tangy Chicken With Parsley And Lime

Prep time: 10 minutes | **Cook time:** 30 minutes | **Serves 2**

- 1 1/2 handful fresh parsley, roughly chopped
- Fresh juice of 1/2 lime
- 1 teaspoon ground black pepper
- 1 1/2 large-sized chicken breasts, cut into halves
- 1 teaspoon kosher salt
- Zest of 1/2 lime

1. Preheat your Air Fryer to 335 degrees F.
2. Toss the chicken breasts with the other ingredients and let it marinate a couple of hours.
3. Roast for 26 minutes and serve warm. Bon appétit!

Chicken Sausage In Dijon Sauce

Prep time: 10 minutes | **Cook time:** 20 minutes | **Serves 4**

- 4 chicken sausages
- 1/4 cup mayonnaise
- 2 tablespoons Dijon mustard
- 1 tablespoon balsamic vinegar
- 1/2 teaspoon dried rosemary

1. Arrange the sausages on the grill pan and transfer it to the preheated Air Fryer.
2. Grill the sausages at 350 degrees F for approximately 13 minutes. Turn them halfway through cooking.
3. Meanwhile, prepare the sauce by mixing the remaining ingredients with a wire whisk. Serve the warm sausages with chilled Dijon sauce. Enjoy!

Paprika Duck

Prep time: 5 minutes | **Cook time:** 28 minutes | **Serves 6**

- 10 oz duck skin
- 1 teaspoon sunflower oil
- ½ teaspoon salt
- ½ teaspoon ground paprika

1. Preheat the air fryer to 375F. Then sprinkle the duck skin with sunflower oil, salt, and ground paprika.
2. Put the duck skin in the air fryer and cook it for 18 minutes.
3. Then flip it on another side and cook for 10 minutes more or until it is crunchy from both sides.

Pesto Chicken

Prep time: 10 minutes | Cook time: 25 minutes | Serves 4

- 12 oz chicken legs
- 1 teaspoon sesame oil
- ½ teaspoon chili flakes
- 4 teaspoons pesto sauce

1. In the shallow bowl mix up pesto sauce, chili flakes, and sesame oil.
2. Then rub the chicken legs with the pesto mixture. Preheat the air fryer to 390F.
3. Put the chicken legs in the air fryer basket and cook them for 25 minutes.

Almond Meatballs

Prep time: 10 minutes | Cook time: 12 minutes | Serves 6

- 16 oz ground chicken
- ½ cup almond flour
- 1 teaspoon salt
- 1 teaspoon ground black pepper
- 1 tablespoon avocado oil

1. Mix ground chicken with almond flour, salt, and ground black pepper.
2. After this, make the meatballs and put them in the air fryer in one layer.
3. Sprinkle the meatballs with avocado oil and cook at 370F for 12 minutes.

Mozzarella Turkey Rolls

Prep time: 10 minutes | Cook time: 10 minutes | Serves 4

- 4 slices turkey breast
- 4 chive shoots (for tying rolls)
- 1 tomato, sliced
- ½ cup basil, fresh, chopped
- 1 cup mozzarella, sliced

1. Preheat your air fryer to 390°Fahrenheit.
2. Place the slices of mozzarella cheese, tomato, and basil onto each slice of turkey. Roll up and tie with chive shoot.
3. Place into air fryer and cook for 10-minutes. Serve warm.

Wine Marinated Turkey Wings

Prep time: 10 minutes | Cook time: 30 minutes | Serves 4

- 1 teaspoon freshly cracked pink peppercorns
- 1½ pound turkey wings, cut into smaller pieces
- 2 teaspoon garlic powder
- 1/3 cup white wine
- 1/2 teaspoon garlic salt
- 1/2 tablespoon coriander, ground

1. Toss all of the above ingredients in a mixing dish. Let it marinate at least 3 hours.
2. Air-fry turkey wings for 28 minutes at 355 degrees F. Bon appétit!

The Super Easy Air Fryer Cookbook | 27

Taco Chicken

Prep time: 15 minutes | Cook time: 30 minutes | Serves 4

- 1 tablespoon taco seasonings
- 1 tablespoon apple cider vinegar
- 2-pounds chicken thighs, skinless, boneless

1. Rub the chicken thighs with taco seasonings and sprinkle with olive oil and apple cider vinegar.
2. Put them in the air fryer and cook at 365F for 15 minutes per side.

Ginger Drumsticks

Prep time: 5 minutes | Cook time: 20 minutes | Serves 4

- 1 teaspoon ground ginger
- ½ teaspoon ground cinnamon
- 1 tablespoon olive oil
- ½ teaspoon onion powder
- 2-pounds chicken drumsticks

1. Mix the chicken drumsticks with onion powder, olive oil, ground cinnamon, and ground ginger.
2. Put them in the air fryer basket and cook at 380F for 20 minutes.

Coriander Chicken Drumsticks

Prep time: 10 minutes | Cook time: 20 minutes | Serves 6

- 6 chicken drumsticks
- 1 tablespoon coconut oil, melted
- 1 tablespoon ground coriander
- 1 teaspoon garlic powder
- ½ teaspoon salt

1. Sprinkle the chicken drumsticks with ground coriander, salt, and garlic powder.
2. Then sprinkle the chicken drumsticks with coconut oil and put it in the air fryer.
3. Cook the meal at 375F for 20 minutes.

Teriyaki Hen Drumsticks

Prep time: 30 minutes | Cook time: 20 minutes | Serves 4

- 6 poultry drumsticks
- 1 mug teriyaki sauce

1. Mix drumsticks with teriyaki sauce in a zip-lock bag. Let the sauce rest for half an hour.
2. Preheat your air fryer to 360ºF.
3. Abode the drumsticks in the air fryer basket and cook for 20 minutes. Shake the basket pair times through food preparation. Garnish with sesame seeds and sliced onions

Faire-Worthy Turkey Legs

Prep time: 5 minutes | Cook time: 27 minutes | Serves 4

- 1 turkey leg
- 1 tsp. olive oil
- 1 tsp. poultry seasoning
- 1 tsp. garlic powder
- salt and black pepper to taste

1. Warm up the air fryer to 350°F for about 4 minutes.
2. Coat the leg with olive oil. Just use your hands and rub them in.
3. In a small bowl, mix the poultry seasoning, garlic powder, salt, and pepper. Rub it on the turkey leg.
4. Coat the inside of the air fryer basket with nonstick spray and place the turkey leg in.
5. Cook for 27 minutes, turning at 14 minutes. Be sure the leg is done by inserting a meat thermometer in the fleshy part of the leg and it should read 165°F.

Turkey Breast

Prep time: 20 minutes | Cook time:35 minutes |Serves 2

4 pound of turkey breast, with the rib removed
2 teaspoons of kosher salt
1/2 tablespoon of dry turkey or poultry seasoning
1 tablespoon of olive oil

1. Coat the turkey breast with 1/2 tablespoon of oil.
2. The next step is to season both sides of the turkey breast with salt and turkey seasoning. You can add the remaining oil to the seasoned turkey.
3. Preheat your air fryer to 350 degrees F before cooking the turkey for 20 minutes.
4. Turn it over and cook it at 160 degrees F for another 30 to 35 minutes.
5. Let it cool for 10 minutes before you carve it.

Bacon-Wrapped Turkey With Cheese

Prep time: 10 minutes | Cook time: 20 minutes | Serves 12

- 1 ½ small-sized turkey breast, chop into 12 pieces
- 12 thin slices Asiago cheese
- Paprika, to taste
- Fine sea salt and ground black pepper, to savor
- 12 rashers bacon

1. Lay out the bacon rashers; place 1 slice of Asiago cheese on each bacon piece.
2. Top with turkey, season with paprika, salt, and pepper, and roll them up; secure with a cocktail stick.
3. Air-fry at 365 degrees F for 13 minutes. Bon appétit!

Almond Coconut Chicken Tenders

Prep time: 5 minutes |Cook time: 20 minutes |Serves 4

- 4 chicken breasts, skinless, boneless and cut into tenders
- a pinch of salt and black pepper
- 1/3 cup almond flour
- 2 eggs, whisked
- 9 ounces coconut flakes

1. Season the chicken tenders with salt and pepper, dredge them in almond flour, then dip in eggs and roll in coconut flakes.
2. Put the chicken tenders in your air fryer's basket and cook at 400 degrees F for 10 minutes on each side.
3. Divide between plates and serve with a side salad.

Easy Blackened Chicken

Prep time: 10 minutes | Cook time: 11 minutes | Serves 2

- 2 medium-sized chicken breasts, skinless and boneless
- 1 tablespoon olive oil
- 3 tablespoons cajun seasoning
- ½ teaspoon salt

1. Rub the chicken breasts with Cajun seasoning, salt, and sprinkle with olive oil. Preheat your air fryer to 370°Fahrenheit and cook chicken breasts for 7-minutes.
2. Turn over and cook for an additional 4-minutes. Slice and serve.

Sweet Chicken Wings

Prep time: 10 minutes | Cook time: 16 minutes | Serves 4

- 1-pound chicken wings
- 1 tablespoon taco seasonings
- 1 tablespoon Erythritol
- 1 tablespoon coconut oil, melted

1. Mix chicken wings with taco seasonings, Erythritol, and coconut oil.
2. Put the chicken wings in the air fryer basket and cook them at 380F for 16 minutes.

Nutmeg Chicken Fillets

Prep time: 15 minutes | Cook time: 12 minutes | Serves 4

- 16 oz chicken fillets
- 1 teaspoon ground nutmeg
- 1 tablespoon avocado oil
- ½ teaspoon salt

1. Mix ground nutmeg with avocado oil and salt.
2. Then rub the chicken fillet with a nutmeg mixture and put it in the air fryer basket.
3. Cook the meal at 385F for 12 minutes.

Tomato Chicken Mix

Prep time: 10 minutes |Cook time: 18 minutes |Serves 4

- 1-pound chicken breast, skinless, boneless
- 1 tablespoon keto tomato sauce
- 1 teaspoon avocado oil
- ½ teaspoon garlic powder

1. In the small bowl mix up tomato sauce, avocado oil, and garlic powder. Then brush the chicken breast with the tomato sauce mixture well.
2. Preheat the air fryer to 385F. Place the chicken breast in the air fryer and cook it for 15 minutes.
3. Then flip it on another side and cook for 3 minutes more. Slice the cooked chicken breast into servings.

Smoked Paprika Chicken

Prep time: 10 minutes | Cook time: 20 minutes | Serves 4

- 2-pounds chicken breast, skinless, boneless
- 1 tablespoon smoked paprika
- 1 teaspoon coconut oil, melted
- 1 tablespoon apple cider vinegar

1. In the shallow bowl, mix coconut oil with apple cider vinegar, and smoked paprika.
2. Carefully brush the chicken breast with smoked paprika mixture.
3. Then put the chicken in the air fryer and cook it at 375F for 20 minutes. Flip the chicken on another side after 10 minutes of cooking.

The Super Easy Air Fryer Cookbook

Chicken Fillet

Prep time: 5 minutes | Cook time: 20 minutes | Serves 4

- 4 chicken fillets
- salt to taste
- 1 garlic clove, crushed
- thyme to taste
- black pepper to taste

1. Add seasoning to fillets, wrapping well for flavor. Heat up the Air Fryer for 5 minutes at 350°F. Place the fillets in the basket, a program for 20 minutes at 350°F.
2. With 5 minutes remaining, turn the fillets and raise the temperature to 390°F.

Pepper Turkey Bacon

Prep time: 10 minutes |Cook time: 8 minutes |Serves 2

- 7 oz turkey bacon
- 1 teaspoon coconut oil, melted
- ½ teaspoon ground black pepper

1. Slice the turkey bacon if needed and sprinkle it with ground black pepper and coconut oil. Preheat the air fryer to 400F.
2. Arrange the turkey bacon in the air fryer in one layer and cook it for 4 minutes.
3. Then flip the bacon on another side and cook for 4 minutes more.

Chapter 4

Beef, Pork and Lamb

Air Fry Rib-Eye Steak

Prep time: 5 minutes | Cook time: 14 minutes | Serves 2

- 2 medium-sized lean rib eye steaks
- Salt & freshly ground black pepper, to taste

1. Let the air fry preheat at 400 F.
2. Season the meat with salt and pepper and put in the air fryer basket. Cook for 14 minutes and flip after half time. Take out from the air fryer and let it rest for 5 minutes. Serve with microgreen salad.

Basil Pork

Prep time: 5 minutes | Cook time: 25 minutes | Serves 4

- 4 pork chops
- a pinch of salt and black pepper
- 2 teaspoons basil, dried
- 2 tablespoons olive oil
- ½ teaspoon chili powder

1. In a pan that fits your air fryer, mix all the ingredients, toss, introduce in the fryer and cook at 400 degrees F for 25 minutes.
2. Divide everything between plates and serve.

Air Fryer Hamburgers

Prep time: 5 minutes | Cook time: 13 minutes | Serves 4

- 4 buns
- 4 cups lean ground beef chuck
- salt to taste
- 4 slices slices of any cheese
- black pepper, to taste

1. Let the air fryer preheat to 350 F.
2. In a bowl, add lean ground beef, pepper, and salt. Mix well and form patties.
3. Put the patties in the air fryer in one layer only, cook for 6 minutes, flip them halfway through. One minute before you take out the patties, add cheese on top. When cheese is melted, take out from the air fryer.
4. Add ketchup, any dressing, tomatoes, lettuce and patties to your buns. Serve hot.

French-Style Smothered Pork Chops

Prep time: 10 minutes | Cook time: 20 minutes | Serves 4

- 2 tablespoons coconut aminos
- 2 tablespoons French wine
- 2 tablespoons rice vinegar
- 1 pound pork loin center rib chops, bone-in
- 1 teaspoon Herbes de Provence
- Celtic salt and ground black pepper, to taste
- 1 tablespoon Dijon mustard

1. Thoroughly combine the coconut aminos, wine, and vinegar; add the pork and let it marinate for 1 hour in the refrigerator.
2. Sprinkle the pork chops with Herbes de Provence, salt, and black pepper. Spread the mustard, all over the pork chops.
3. Cook in the preheated Air Fryer at 400 degrees F for 12 minutes. Serve warm with mashed potatoes if desired.

Onion Beef Bites

Prep time: 10 minutes | Cook time: 30 minutes | Serves 4

- 2-pound beef fillet
- 1 tablespoon onion powder
- ¼ cup heavy cream
- ½ teaspoon salt
- 1 teaspoon olive oil

1. Cut the beef fillet into bites and sprinkle with onion powder and salt.
2. Then put the beef bites in the air fryer and add heavy cream.
3. Cook the beef bites at 360F for 15 minutes per side.

Bacon With Shallot And Greens

Prep time: 10 minutes | Cook time: 10 minutes | Serves 2

- 7 ounces mixed greens
- 8 thick slices pork bacon
- 2 shallots, peeled and diced
- Nonstick cooking spray

1. Begin by preheating the air fryer to 345 degrees F.
2. Now, add the shallot and bacon to the Air Fryer cooking basket; set the timer for 2 minutes. Spritz with a nonstick cooking spray.
3. After that, pause the Air Fryer; throw in the mixed greens; give it a good stir and cook an additional 5 minutes. Serve warm.

Mustard Pork

Prep time: 5 minutes |Cook time: 30 minutes |Serves 4

- 1 pound pork tenderloin, trimmed
- a pinch of salt and black pepper
- 2 tablespoons olive oil
- 3 tablespoons mustard
- 2 tablespoons balsamic vinegar

1. In a bowl, mix the pork tenderloin with the rest of the ingredients and rub well.
2. Put the roast in your air fryer's basket and cook at 380 degrees F for 30 minutes.
3. Slice the roast, divide between plates and serve.

Air Fryer Pork Taquitos

Prep time: 10 minutes | Cook time: 7 to 10 minutes | Serves 2

3 cups shredded cooked pork tenderloin
Spray cooking oil on
2 ½ fat-free shredded mozzarella
10 mini tortillas.
1 tsp lime juice

1. Preheat the air fryer to 380 degrees Fahrenheit.
2. Combine the lime juice and the meat.
3. To soften the tortilla, microwave it for 10 seconds with a moist cloth over it.
4. Place the pork filling and cheese on top of a tortilla and wrap it up firmly.
5. Arrange tortillas on a foil-lined baking sheet.
6. Spray the tortillas with oil. Cook for 7 to 10 minutes, or until golden brown, flipping halfway through.
7. Serve with a fresh salad on the side.

Tomato Rib Eye Steaks

Prep time: 10 minutes | Cook time: 24 minutes | Serves 4

- 3-pound rib-eye steak
- 1 tablespoon keto tomato paste
- 1 tablespoon avocado oil
- 1 teaspoon salt
- 1 teaspoon cayenne pepper

1. In the shallow bowl, mix tomato paste with avocado oil, salt, and cayenne pepper.
2. Then run the beef with tomato mixture and put it in the air fryer.
3. Cook the meal at 380F for 12 minutes per side.

Fried Pork Chops

Prep time: 5 minutes | Cook time: 35 minutes | Serves 2

- 3 cloves ground garlic
- 2 tbsps. olive oil
- 1 tbsp. of marinade
- 4 thawed pork chops

1. In a bowl, mix the cloves of ground garlic, oil, and marinade.
2. Apply the mixture on the pork chops.
3. Put the chops in the air fryer and cook at 360 C for 35 minutes.

Lamb Chops With Herb Butter

Prep time: 10 minutes | Cook time: 5 minutes | Serves 4

- 4 lamb chops
- 1 tsp. rosemary, diced
- 1 tbsp. butter
- Pepper
- Salt

1. Season lamb chops with pepper and salt.
2. Place the dehydrating tray in a multi-level air fryer basket. Insert the basket in the air fryer oven.
3. Place the lamb chops on dehydrating tray.
4. Seal pot with the air fryer lid and select "Air Fry" mode, then set the temperature to 400°F and cook for 5 minutes.
5. Stir in rosemary and butter and spread overcooked lamb chops. Serve and enjoy.

Garlic Pork Chops

Prep time: 5 minutes | Cook time: 25 minutes | Serves 4

- 2 tablespoons olive oil
- 4 pork chops
- a pinch of salt and black pepper
- 4 garlic cloves, minced
- 3 tablespoons cider vinegar

1. Heat up a pan that fits the air fryer with the oil over medium-high heat, add the pork chops and brown for 5 minutes.
2. Add the rest of the ingredients, toss, put the pan in your air fryer and cook at 400 degrees F for 20 minutes. Divide between plates and serve.

Hot Dogs

Prep time: 2 minutes | Cook time: 10 minutes | Serves 4

- 4 beef hot dogs

1. Using a knife, score the hot dogs to create several little slits to prevent bursting during cooking.
2. Lay the hotdogs in the air fryer. Bake for 5 minutes at 375°F.
3. When the timer is up, rotate the hotdogs; cook for 3 minutes more.
4. Remove from fryer and dig in.

Pork Bondiola Chop

Prep time: 5 minutes | Cook time: 20 minutes |Serves 4

- 1kg bondiola in pieces
- Breadcrumbs
- 2 beaten eggs
- Seasoning to taste

1. Cut the bondiola into small pieces
2. Add seasonings to taste.
3. Pour the beaten eggs on the seasoned bondiola.
4. Add the breadcrumbs.
5. Cook in the air fryer for 20 minutes while turning the food halfway.
6. Serve.

Parmesan Beef Meatballs

Prep time: 15 minutes | Cook time: 8 minutes | Serves 6

- 2-pounds ground beef
- 1 tablespoon taco seasonings
- 2 oz Parmesan, grated
- 1 teaspoon olive oil

1. Brush the air fryer basket with olive oil.
2. Then mix all remaining ingredients and make the meatballs.
3. Put the meatballs in the air fryer basket and cook them at 390F for 4 minutes per side.

Beef Empanadas

Prep time: 10 minutes | Cook time: 20 minutes |Serves 3

- 8 Goya empanada discs, defrosted
- 1 cup picadillo
- 1 egg white, blended
- 1 tsp. water
- Cooking spray

1. Set air fryer at 325 degrees F.
2. Apply a cooking spray to the basket.
3. Place 2 tbsps. of picadillo to each disc space. Fold in half and secure using a fork. Do the same for all the dough.
4. Mix water and egg whites. Sprinkle to empanadas top.
5. Set 3 of them in your air fryer and allow to bake for minutes. Set aside and do the same for the remaining empanadas.

Vinegar Pork Chops

Prep time: 10 minutes | Cook time: 20 minutes | Serves 4

- 4 pork chops
- ¼ cup apple cider vinegar
- 1 teaspoon ground black pepper
- 1 teaspoon olive oil

1. Mix apple cider vinegar with olive oil and ground black pepper.
2. Then mix pork chops with apple cider vinegar mixture.
3. Put the meat in the air fryer and cook it at 375F for 10 minutes per side.

The Super Easy Air Fryer Cookbook

Crunchy Canadian Bacon

Prep time: 10 minutes | Cook time: 10 minutes | Serves 4

- 10-ounces canadian bacon, sliced
- 1 teaspoon cream
- ½ teaspoon salt
- ¼ teaspoon ground black pepper
- ½ teaspoon ground coriander
- ½ teaspoon ground thyme

1. In a mixing bowl combine the thyme, coriander, black pepper, and salt. Sprinkle this spice mix on top of the bacon slices on each side. Preheat your air fryer to 360°Fahrenheit.
2. Place prepared bacon inside the air fryer and cook it for 5-minutes. After this turn, the sliced bacon over and cook for an additional 5-minutes more. Once the bacon is cooked, remove it from air fryer and sprinkle it with cream and serve immediately!

Beef & Mushrooms

Prep time: 10 minutes | Cook time: 10 minutes | Serves 1

- 6-ounces of beef
- ¼ onion, diced
- 2 tablespoons of favorite marinade
- ½ cup mushroom slices

1. Cut beef strips or cubes and place in a bowl. Coat the meat with marinade and cover bowl.
2. Place in the fridge for about 3-hours. Put the meat into a baking dish and add onion and mushrooms. Air fry at 350°Fahrenheit for 10-minutes. Serve warm.

Classic Keto Cheeseburgers

Prep time: 10 minutes | Cook time: 15 minutes | Serves 4

- 1 ½ pounds ground chuck
- 1 envelope onion soup mix
- Kosher salt and freshly ground black pepper, to taste
- 1 teaspoon paprika
- 4 slices Monterey-Jack cheese

1. In a mixing dish, thoroughly combine ground chuck, onion soup mix, salt, black pepper, and paprika.
2. Next step, place the slices of cheese on the top of the warm burgers. Air-fry for one minute more.
3. Serve with mustard and pickled salad of choice. Bon appétit!

Ginger Lamb

Prep time: 10 minutes | Cook time: 30 minutes | Serves 2

- 15 oz lamb sirloin
- 1 tablespoon avocado oil
- 1 teaspoon ginger powder
- ½ teaspoon onion powder
- 1 teaspoon keto tomato paste

1. Rub the lamb sirloin with ginger powder and onion powder.
2. Then mix avocado oil with tomato paste.
3. Brush the lamb sirloin with tomato mixture and put it in the air fryer basket.
4. Cook the meal at 360F for 30 minutes.

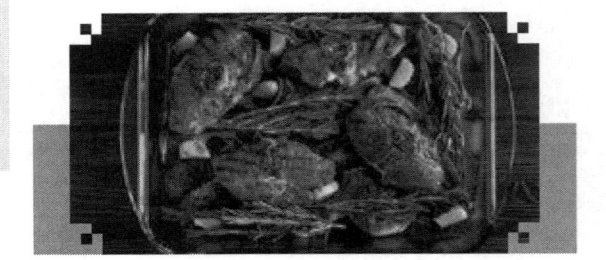

Coconut Beef Steak

Prep time: 10 minutes | Cook time: 16 minutes | Serves 4

- 2-pounds beef steak
- 3 tablespoons coconut oil
- 1 teaspoon coconut shred
- 1 teaspoon dried basil

1. Rub the beef steak with coconut shred and dried basil.
2. Then brush the beef steak with coconut oil and put it in the air fryer.
3. Cook the beef steak at 390F for 8 minutes per side.

Jamaican Pork With Jerk

Prep time: 10 minutes | Cook time: 20 minutes | Serves 4

- pork, cut into three-inch pieces
- ¼ cup Jerk paste

1. Rub jerk paste all over the pork pieces. Let it marinate for four hours in the refrigerator.
2. Let the air fryer preheat to 390°F. spray with olive oil.
3. Before putting in the air fryer, let the meat sit for 20 minutes at room temperature.
4. Cook for 20 minutes at 390°F in the air fryer, flip halfway through.
5. Take out from the air fryer and let it rest for ten minutes before slicing. Serve with microgreens.

Thyme and Turmeric Pork

Prep time: 10 minutes |Cook time: 15 minutes |Serves 4

- 1-pound pork tenderloin
- ½ teaspoon salt
- ½ teaspoon ground turmeric
- 1 tablespoon dried thyme
- 1 tablespoon avocado oil

1. Rub the pork tenderloin with salt, ground turmeric, and dried thyme. Then brush it with avocado oil. Preheat the air fryer to 370F.
2. Place the pork tenderloin in the air fryer basket and cook it for 15 minutes. You can flip the meat on another side during cooking if desired.

Smoked Pork

Prep time: 20 minutes |Cook time: 20 minutes |Serves 5

- 1-pound pork shoulder
- 1 tablespoon liquid smoke
- 1 tablespoon olive oil
- 1 teaspoon salt

1. Mix up liquid smoke, salt, and olive oil in the shallow bowl.
2. Then carefully brush the pork shoulder with the liquid smoke mixture from each side.
3. Make the small cuts in the meat. Preheat the air fryer to 390F. Put the pork shoulder in the air fryer basket and cook the meat for 10 minutes.
4. After this, flip the meat on another side and cook it for 10 minutes more. Let the cooked pork shoulder rest for 10-15 minutes. Shred it with the help of 2 forks.

Taco Pork

Prep time: 10 minutes | Cook time: 30 minutes | Serves 6

- 4-pound pork stew meat
- 1 tablespoon taco seasonings
- 1 tablespoon coconut oil, melted

1. Chop the pork stew meat and put it in the skillet.
2. Add coconut oil and roast the meat for 3 minutes per side.
3. Then mix meat with taco seasonings and put in the air fryer.
4. Cook the meat at 365F for 25 minutes.

Cheesy Pork Chops In Air Fryer

Prep time: 5 minutes | Cook time: 8 minutes | Serves 2

- 4 lean pork chops
- ½ tsp. salt
- ½ tsp. garlic powder
- 4 tbsp. shredded cheese
- chopped cilantro

1. Let the air fryer preheat to 350F.
2. Rub the pork chops with garlic, cilantro, and salt. Put in the air fryer and let it cook for four minutes.
3. Flip them and cook for two minutes more.
4. Add cheese on top and cook for another two minutes or until the cheese is melted.
5. Serve with salad greens.

Pork Rind

Prep time: 9 minutes | Cook time: 50 minutes | Serves 4

- 1 kg pork rinds
- Salt to taste
- 1/2 tsp. black pepper

1. Preheat the air fryer. Set the time to 5 minutes and the temperature to 380°F.
2. Cut the bacon into cubes 1 finger wide. Season with salt and a pinch of pepper.
3. Place in the basket of the air fryer. Set the time to 45 minutes and press the POWER button.
4. Shake the basket every 10 minutes so that the pork rinds stay golden brown equally.
5. Once they are ready, drain a little on the paper towel so they stay dry. Transfer to a plate and serve.

Chapter 5

Fish & Seafood

Asian Sesame Cod

Prep time: 5 minutes | Cook time: 10 minutes | Serves 1

- 1 tablespoon reduced-sodium soy sauce
- 2 teaspoons honey
- 1 teaspoon sesame seeds
- 6 ounces (170 g) cod fillet

1. In a lesser bowl, syndicate the soy sauce and honey.
2. Sprig the air fryer basket with nonstick cooking spray, then place the fish in the basket, brush with the soy mixture, and sprinkle with sesame seeds. Roast at 360°F for 10 minutes or until opaque.
3. Remove the fryer's fish and allow cooling on a wire rack for 5 minutes before serving.

Breaded Hake With Green Chili Pepper

Prep time: 15 minutes | Cook time: 30 minutes | Serves 4

- 4 breaded hake fillets
- 8 tsps. mayonnaise
- green mojito
- 8 tsps. extra virgin olive oil

1. Paint the breaded hake fillets with extra virgin olive oil.
2. Prepare air fryer and put in the basket. Cook at 180 C for 30 minutes.
3. Meanwhile, put in a bowl 8 teaspoons of mayonnaise and 2 of green mojito.
4. Serve the breaded hake fillets with the green mojito mayonnaise.

Air Fryer Salmon Cakes

Prep time: 9 minutes | Cook time: 7 minutes | Serves 2

- Fresh salmon fillet (8 oz.)
- 1 egg
- 1/8 salt
- 1/4 tablespoon garlic powder
- 1 sliced lemon

1. In a mixing dish, combine the salmon, egg, and seasonings.
2. Make small cakes.
3. Preheat the air fryer to 390 degrees Fahrenheit. Add sliced lemons to the bottom of the air fryer dish; place cakes on top.
4. Bake for 7 minutes. Eat it with your preferred dip according to your dietary needs.

Air Fried Cajun Salmon

Prep time: 10 minutes | Cook time: 7 minutes | Serves 1

- 1 fresh salmon
- 1 tbsp. Cajun seasoning
- 1 lemon juice

1. Let the air fryer preheat to 375°F.
2. Pat dries the salmon fillet. Rub lemon juice and Cajun seasoning over the fish fillet.
3. Place in the air fryer and cook for 7 minutes.

Tuna Melt

Prep time: 7 minutes | Cook time: 8 minutes | Serves 1

- 2 slices sandwich bread
- temperature butter
- 1/2 cup tuna salad
- 1-2 tablespoons mayonnaise
- 1 1/2-2 slices Cheddar cheese

1. First, cover one side of bread with the mayo or room temp butter. Place that piece of bread into the air fryer basket, mayo-side down.
2. Next, put cheese slices on top of the bread. Use a spoon to push out the tuna salad so that it goes around each slice of cheese.
3. Finally, add one more piece of bread and coat one side in mayonnaise just like the other side.
4. Shut off the air fryer and set it to cook at 380°F for 8 minutes; then flip it over halfway through cooking time so that both sides are golden brown with melted cheese.
5. Remove from the basket and cut in half on a cutting board while still warm!

Restaurant-Style Flounder Cutlets

Prep time: 10 minutes | Cook time: 15 minutes | Serves 2

- 1 egg
- 1 cup Pecorino Romano cheese, grated
- Sea salt and white pepper, to taste
- 1/2 teaspoon cayenne pepper
- 1 teaspoon dried parsley flakes
- 2 flounder fillets

1. To make a breading station, whisk the egg until frothy.
2. In another bowl, mix Pecorino Romano cheese, and spices.
3. Dip the fish in the egg mixture and turn to coat evenly; then, dredge in the cracker crumb mixture, turning a couple of times to coat evenly.
4. Cook in the preheated Air Fryer at 390 degrees F for 5 minutes; turn them over and cook another 5 minutes. Enjoy!

The Super Easy Air Fryer Cookbook | 43

Oregano Fish Sticks

Prep time: 15 minutes | Cook time: 10 minutes | Serves 4

- 8 oz cod fillet
- 1 egg, beaten
- 2 tablespoons coconut shred
- 1 teaspoon dried oregano
- ½ teaspoon salt
- 1 teaspoon avocado oil

1. Cut the cod fillet into sticks.
2. Then mix salt with dried oregano and coconut shred.
3. Dip the cod sticks in the beaten egg and coat in the coconut shred mixture.
4. Sprinkle the cod sticks with avocado oil and cook in the air fryer at 400F for 10 minutes.

Bacon Scallops

Prep time: 15 minutes | Cook time: 7 minutes | Serves 4

- 1-pound scallops
- 4 oz bacon, sliced
- 1 teaspoon avocado oil
- 1 teaspoon chili powder

1. Wrap the scallops in the bacon and sprinkle with avocado oil and chili powder.
2. Put the scallops in the air fryer and cook them at 400F for 7 minutes.

Miso Fish

Prep time: 10 minutes | Cook time:10 minutes |Serves 2

- 2 cod fish fillets
- 1 tbsp garlic, chopped
- 2 tsp swerve
- 2 tbsp miso

1. Add all ingredients to the Ziplock bag. Shake well place in the refrigerator overnight.
2. Place marinated fish fillets into the air fryer basket and cooked at 350 F for 10 minutes.
3. Serve and enjoy.

Crunchy Red Fish

Prep time: 15 minutes | Cook time: 8 minutes | Serves 4

- 2-pound salmon fillet
- ¼ cup coconut shred
- 2 eggs, beaten
- 1 teaspoon coconut oil
- 1 teaspoon Italian seasonings

1. Cut the salmon fillet into servings.
2. Then sprinkle the fish with Italian seasonings and dip in the eggs.
3. After this, coat every salmon fillet in coconut shred and put it in the air fryer.
4. Cook the fish at 375F for 4 minutes per side.

The Super Easy Air Fryer Cookbook

Breaded Fish

Prep time: 10 minutes | Cook time: 12 minutes | Serves 4

- 4 fish fillets
- 1 egg
- 5-ounces breadcrumbs
- 4 tablespoons olive oil

1. Preheat your air fryer to 350°Fahrenheit. In a bowl mix oil and breadcrumbs. Whisk egg.
2. Gently dip the fish into egg and then into crumb mixture. Put into air fryer and cook for 12-minutes.

Crumbed Fish

Prep time: 10 minutes | Cook time:12 minutes |Serves 2

- 1 mug completely dry breadcrumbs
- 1/4 mug vegetable oil
- 4 go to pieces fillets
- 1 beaten egg
- 1 sliced lemon.

1. Preheat an air fryer to 351ºF.
2. Mix breadcrumbs and oil with each other in a dish. Mix up until blend comes to be loosened as well as crumbly.
3. Dip fish fillets right into the egg; shake off any type of unwanted. Dip fillets into the bread crumb mix; layer uniformly as well as completely.
4. Lay coated fillets carefully in the preheated air fryer. Prepare up until fish flakes quickly with a fork, about 12 mins.
5. Garnish with lemon pieces.

Lime-Garlic Shrimp Kebabs

Prep time: 5 minutes | Cook time: 8 minutes | Serves 2

- 1 lime
- 1 cup raw shrimp
- 1/8 teaspoon salt
- 1 clove of garlic
- Freshly ground black pepper

1. In water, let wooden skewers soak for 20 minutes.
2. Let the Air fryer preheat to 350°F.
3. In a bowl, mix shrimp, minced garlic, lime juice, kosher salt, and pepper.
4. Add shrimp on skewers. Place skewers in the air fryer, and cook for 8 minutes. Turn halfway over.

Air Fried Salmon Cakes

Prep time: 9 minutes | Cook time: 7 minutes | Serves 2

- 8 oz. fresh salmon fillet
- 1 egg
- ⅛ salt
- ¼ garlic powder
- 1 Sliced lemon

1. Let the air fryer preheat to 390°F.
2. In a bowl, chop the salmon, add the egg and spices. Form tiny cakes.
3. On the bottom of the air fryer bowl, arrange the sliced lemons and place cakes on top. Cook for 7 minutes.

Rosemary Shrimp Skewers

Prep time: 10 minutes | Cook time: 5 minutes | Serves 5

- 4-pounds shrimps, peeled
- 1 tablespoon dried rosemary
- 1 tablespoon avocado oil
- 1 teaspoon apple cider vinegar

1. Mix the shrimps with dried rosemary, avocado oil, and apple cider vinegar.
2. Then sting the shrimps into skewers and put in the air fryer.
3. Cook the shrimps at 400F for 5 minutes.

Sesame Seeds Coated Tuna

Prep time: 10 minutes | Cook time: 10 minutes | Serves 2

- 1 egg white
- 1/4 cup white sesame seeds
- 1 tbsp. black sesame seeds
- Salt and ground black pepper
- 6-oz. tuna steaks

1. Get a shallow bowl, beat the egg white.
2. In another bowl, mix the sesame seeds, salt, and black pepper.
3. Dip the tuna steaks into the egg white and then coat with the sesame seeds mixture.
4. Press the "power button" of air fry oven and turn the dial to select the "air fry" mode.
5. Press the time button and set the cooking time to 6 minutes.
6. Now push the temp button and rotate the dial to set the temperature at 400°F.
7. Press the "start/pause" button to start.
8. When the unit beeps to show that it is preheated, open the lid.
9. Arrange the tuna steaks in greased "air fry basket" and insert in the oven.
10. Flip the tuna steaks once halfway through.
11. Serve hot.

The Super Easy Air Fryer Cookbook

Parmesan Walnut Salmon

Prep time: 10 minutes | Cook time: 12 minutes | Serves 4

- 4 salmon fillets
- 1/4 cup parmesan cheese, grated
- 1/2 cup walnuts
- 1 tsp olive oil
- 1 tbsp lemon rind

1. Preheat the air fryer to 370 F.
2. Spray an air fryer baking dish with cooking spray.
3. Place salmon on a baking dish.
4. Add walnuts into the food processor and process until finely ground.
5. Mix ground walnuts with parmesan cheese, oil, and lemon rind. Stir well.
6. Spoon walnut mixture over the salmon and press gently.
7. Cook for 12 minutes.
8. Serve and enjoy.

Onion Shrimps

Prep time: 10 minutes | Cook time: 5 minutes | Serves 3

- 1-pound shrimps, peeled
- 1 teaspoon onion powder
- 1 teaspoon avocado oil
- ½ teaspoon salt

1. Sprinkle the shrimps with onion powder, avocado oil, and salt.
2. Put the shrimps in the air fryer and cook at 400F for 5 minutes.

Sweet Tilapia Fillets

Prep time: 5 minutes | Cook time: 14 minutes | Serves 4

- 2 tablespoons Erythritol
- 1 tablespoon apple cider vinegar
- 4 tilapia fillets, boneless
- 1 teaspoon olive oil

1. Mix apple cider vinegar with olive oil and Erythritol.
2. Then rub the tilapia fillets with the sweet mixture and put in the air fryer basket in one layer.
3. Cook the fish at 360F for 7 minutes per side.

Salmon With Honey Glaze

Prep time: 11 minutes | Cook time: 16 minutes | Serves 2

- 6 tablespoons of gluten-free soy sauce
- Salmon fillets, 2 pcs.
- 3 tablespoons of sweet rice wine.
- 1 tablespoon water
- 6 teaspoons of honey

1. Combine sweet rice wine, soy sauce, honey, and water in a mixing dish.
2. Set aside half of it.
3. Marinate the fish for 2 hours in half of the sauce.
4. Preheat the air fryer to 180 degrees Celsius.
5. Cook for 8 minutes, turning halfway through, and cook for 5 minute more.
6. After 3 or 4 minutes, baste the salmon with the marinade mixture.
7. Pour half of the marinade into a skillet and reduce to half before serving with a sauce.

Air-Fried Cajun Shrimp

Prep time: 10 minutes | Cook time: 5 minutes | Serves 4

- 1 ¼ lbs. shrimp, peeled and deveined
- ¼ teaspoon salt
- ½ teaspoon paprika
- 1 tablespoon olive oil
- ¼ cayenne pepper
- ½ teaspoon old bay seasoning

1. Preheat air fryer to 400°Fahrenheit. Mix all the ingredients in a bowl.
2. Place the seasoned shrimp into air fryer basket and cook for 5-minutes.

Nacho-Crusted Shrimp

Prep time: 10 minutes | Cook time: 8 minutes | Serves 8

- 18 jumbo shrimps, peeled and deveined
- 1 egg, beaten
- 8-9-ounce nacho-flavored chips, crushed
- salt and pepper to taste

1. Prepare two shallow dishes, one with egg and one with crushed chips. Season with a pinch of salt and pepper. Dip shrimp in the egg and then coat in nacho crumbs.
2. Preheat your air fryer to 350°Fahrenheit. Arrange the shrimp in air fryer and cook for 8-minutes.

Air Fried Catfish

Prep time: 5 minutes | Cook time: 20 minutes | Serves 4

- 4 catfish fillet
- 1 tbsp. olive oil
- 1/4 cup fish seasoning
- 1 tbsp. fresh parsley, chopped
- Cooking spray

1. Preheat the air fryer to 400°F. Spray the air fryer basket with cooking spray.
2. Season the fish with seasoning and place it into the air fryer basket.
3. Turn the fish to another side and cook for 10 more minutes. Garnish with parsley and serve.

Salmon With Maple Soy Glaze

Prep time: 5 minutes | Cook time: 8 minutes | Serves 4

- 3 tablespoon pure maple syrup
- 1 tablespoon sriracha hot sauce
- 4 wild salmon fillets, skinless
- 3 tablespoon reduced sodium soy sauce
- 1 clove garlic

1. Combine maple syrup, soy sauce, sriracha, and garlic in a small bowl.
1. Pour into a gallon-sized re-sealable bag and add the salmon.
2. Marinate for 20 to 30 minutes, turning once or twice. Lightly spray the basket with oil. Remove fish from marinade and pat dry with paper towels.
3. Place fish in an air fryer basket at 400°F for 7-8 minutes or longer, depending on the thickness of salmon.
4. Meanwhile, bring marinade to a simmer over medium-low heat; reduce until thickened into glaze; spoon over fish just before eating.

Air-Fried Crumbed Fish

Prep time: 10 minutes | Cook time: 12 minutes | Serves 2

- 4 fish fillets
- 4 tbsp. olive oil
- 1 egg beaten
- 1/4 cup whole-wheat breadcrumbs

1. Let the air fryer preheat to 375°F.
2. In a bowl, mix breadcrumbs with oil. Mix well.
3. First, coat the fish in the egg mix (egg beaten with water) than in the breadcrumb mix. Coat well.
4. Place in the air fryer and let it cook for 12 minutes. Serve hot with salad green and lemon.

Blackened Salmon

Prep time: 10 minutes | Cook time: 8 minutes | Serves 2

- 10 oz salmon fillet
- ½ teaspoon ground coriander
- 1 teaspoon ground cumin
- 1 teaspoon dried basil
- 1 tablespoon avocado oil

1. In the shallow bowl, mix ground coriander, ground cumin, and dried basil.
2. Then coat the salmon fillet in the spices and sprinkle with avocado oil.
3. Put the fish in the air fryer basket and cook at 395F for 4 minutes per side.

Air Fryer Salmon With Maple Soy Glaze

Prep time: 6 minutes | Cook time: 8 minutes | Serves 4

- 1 tbsp. pure maple syrup
- 3 tbsp. gluten-free soy sauce
- 1 tbsp. sriracha hot sauce
- 2 garlic cloves, minced
- 4 fillets salmon, skinless

1. In a Ziploc bag, mix sriracha, maple syrup, garlic, and soy sauce with salmon.
2. Mix well and let it marinate for at least 30 minutes.
3. Let the air fryer preheat to 400°F and spray the basket with oil.
4. Take fish out from the marinade, pat dry. Put the salmon in the air fryer, cook for 8 minutes or longer.
5. In the meantime, in a saucepan, add the marinade, let it simmer until reduced to half. Add the glaze over the salmon and serve.

The Super Easy Air Fryer Cookbook

Chapter 6

Side Dishes and Snacks

Mini Pizza

Prep time: 2 minutes | Cook time: 5 minutes | Serves 1

- 1/4 cup sliced olives
- 1 pita bread
- 1 tomato
- 1/2 cup shredded cheese

1. Let the air fryer preheat to 350 F.
2. Lay pita flat on a plate. Add cheese, slices of tomatoes, and olives.
3. Cook for five minutes at 350 F.

Mozzarella Snack

Prep time: 5 minutes | Cook time: 5 minutes | Serves 8

- 2 cups mozzarella, shredded
- ¾ cup almond flour
- 2 teaspoons psyllium husk powder
- ¼ teaspoon sweet paprika

1. Put the mozzarella in a bowl, melt it in the microwave for 2 minutes, add all the other ingredients quickly and stir really until you obtain a dough.
2. Divide the dough into 2 balls, roll them on 2 baking sheets and cut into triangles.
3. Arrange the tortillas in your air fryer's basket and bake at 370 degrees F for 5 minutes.
4. Transfer to bowls and serve as a snack.

Cheesy Bell Pepper Eggs

Prep time: 10 minutes | Cook time: 15 minutes | Serves 4

- 4 medium green bell peppers
- 3 ounces cooked ham, chopped
- 1/4 medium onion, peeled and chopped
- 8 large eggs
- 1 cup mild Cheddar cheese

1. Cut each bell pepper from its tops. Pick the seeds with a small knife and the white membranes. Place onion and ham into each pepper.
2. Break two eggs into each chili pepper. Cover with 1/4 cup of peppered cheese. Put the basket into the air fryer.
3. Set the temperature to 390 °F and change the timer for 15 minutes.
4. Peppers will be tender when fully fried, and the eggs will be solid. Serve hot.

Potato Chips

Prep time: 20 minutes | Cook time: 15 minutes | Serves 2

- minced fresh parsley
- 1/4 teaspoon sea salt
- 1 large potato
- olive oil-flavored cooking spray

1. Preheat the air fryer to 360°F. Use a vegetable peeler and cut potatoes into very thin slices. Transfer to a large bowl; add enough ice water to cover them. Soak for 15 minutes; drain them, add more ice water, and soak another 15 minutes.
2. Drain potatoes; place on towels to pat dry. Spritz them with cooking spray; sprinkle with salt. In batches, place potato slices in a single layer on greased trays in the air fryer basket.
3. Cook until crisp and golden brown, stirring and turning every 5-7 minutes if necessary. Sprinkle it with parsley if you feel like it.

Coriander Fennel

Prep time: 5 minutes | Cook time: 15 minutes | Serves 4

- 1 pound fennel bulb, cut into small wedges
- 1 teaspoon ground coriander
- 1 tablespoon avocado oil
- ½ teaspoon salt

1. Rub the fennel bulb with ground coriander, avocado oil, and salt.
2. Put it in the air fryer basket and cook at 390F for 15 minutes. Flip the fennel on another side after 7 minutes of cooking.

Broccoli Hash Brown

Prep time: 5 minutes | Cook time: 15 minutes | Serves 4

- 2 cups broccoli, chopped
- 3 eggs, whisked
- 1 tablespoon coconut oil
- 1 teaspoon dried oregano

1. Mix broccoli with eggs and put the mixture in the air fryer.
2. Add coconut oil and dried oregano.
3. Cook the meal at 400F for 15 minutes. Stir the meal every 5 minutes.

Cabbage Steaks

Prep time: 10 minutes | Cook time: 25 minutes | Serves 4

- 1-pound white cabbage, cut into steaks
- 1 tablespoon avocado oil
- 1 teaspoon salt
- 1 teaspoon apple cider vinegar
- ½ teaspoon mustard

1. Rub the white cabbage steaks with avocado oil, salt, apple cider vinegar, and mustard.
2. Then put them in the air fryer basket in one layer and cook at 375F for 15 minutes.
3. After this, flip the cabbage steaks on another side and cook them for 10 minutes more.

Broccoli Tots

Prep time: 15 minutes | Cook time: 8 minutes | Serves 4

- 1 teaspoon mascarpone
- 5 oz Cheddar cheese, shredded
- 3 cups broccoli, chopped, boiled
- ¼ teaspoon onion powder
- 1 teaspoon avocado oil

1. In the mixing bowl mix mascarpone with Cheddar cheese, broccoli, and onion powder.
2. Make the broccoli tots from the mixture and put them in the air fryer basket in one layer.
3. Sprinkle the broccoli tots with avocado oil and cook them at 400F for 8 minutes.

Turmeric Cauliflower Rice

Prep time: 5 minutes | Cook time: 20 minutes | Serves 4

- 3 cups cauliflower, shredded
- 1 tablespoon coconut oil
- 1 teaspoon ground turmeric
- ½ teaspoon dried oregano

1. Grease the air fryer basket with coconut oil.
2. Then mix cauliflower with ground turmeric and dried oregano. Put the mixture in the air fryer.
3. Cook the cauliflower rice at 360F for 20 minutes. Shake the rice from time to time to avoid burning.

Air Fryer Squash

Prep time: 5 minutes | Cook time: 10 minutes | Serves 2

- 1/2 tablespoon olive oil
- 1 delicata squash
- 1/2 teaspoon salt
- 1/2 teaspoon rosemary

1. Chop the squash in slices of 1/4 thickness. Discard the seeds.
2. In a bowl, add olive oil, rosemary, salt, with squash slices. Mix well.
3. Cook the squash for ten minutes at 400 F, flipping the squash halfway through.

Eggplant Mash

Prep time: 10 minutes | Cook time: 15 minutes | Serves 4

- ½ cup Mozzarella, shredded
- 2 eggplants, trimmed
- 1 tablespoon avocado oil
- ½ teaspoon dried cilantro

1. Chop the eggplants and sprinkle them with avocado oil.
2. Cook the vegetables in the air fryer for 15 minutes.
3. Then transfer them in the blender. Add cilantro and cheese.
4. Blend the mixture until smooth.

Spicy Green Beans

Prep time: 10 minutes | Cook time: 10 minutes | Serves 2

- 6 ounces green beans
- 1 tablespoon olive oil
- ½ teaspoon chili garlic paste
- ½ tablespoon panko bread crumbs
- 1/8 teaspoon salt

1. In a small mixing bowl, add olive oil, chili garlic paste, and panko bread crumbs and mix them. Add salt to taste. And toss green beans in it.
2. Place the green beans in a mesh basket and place it inside the air fryer.
3. Set temperature to 400° F and cook for 4 minutes.
4. Shake basket after 4 minutes; continue to cook for 5 to 7 more minutes or until desired doneness is achieved.
5. Serve warm.

Pumpkin Skinny Chips

Prep time: 20 minutes | Cook time: 13 minutes | Serves 2

- 1 pound of pumpkin, divided into sticks.
- Coconut oil, 1 tablespoon
- 1/2 tablespoon rosemary
- 1/2 tablespoon basil
- To taste, add salt and black pepper.

1. Preheat the air fryer to 395 degrees Fahrenheit. Coconut oil should be used to rub the pumpkin sticks before adding the spices and combining.
2. Cook the basket for 13 minutes, shaking halfway through.
3. Add the mayonnaise to the dish. Enjoy!

Turmeric Tempeh

Prep time: 8 minutes | Cook time: 12 minutes | Serves 4

- 1 teaspoon apple cider vinegar
- 1 tablespoon avocado oil
- ¼ teaspoon ground turmeric
- 6 oz tempeh, chopped

1. Mix avocado oil with apple cider vinegar and ground turmeric.
2. Then sprinkle the tempeh with turmeric mixture and put it in the air fryer basket.
3. Cook the tempeh at 350F for 12 minutes. Shake it after 6 minutes of cooking.

Keto Coleslaw

Prep time: 10 minutes | Cook time: 20 minutes | Serves 4

- 1 cup white cabbage, shredded
- 2 tablespoons apple cider vinegar
- ½ cup heavy cream
- 1 teaspoon ground black pepper
- 1 tablespoon Dijon mustard

1. Mix white cabbage with heavy cream and put it in the air fryer basket.
2. Cook the cabbage for 20 minutes at 350F. Stir it from time to time.
3. Then transfer the white cabbage mixture in the salad bowl.
4. Add all remaining ingredients and carefully mix.

Rutabaga Bites

Prep time: 10 minutes | Cook time: 20 minutes | Serves 4

- 15 ounces rutabaga, cut into fries
- 4 tablespoons avocado oil
- 1 teaspoon garlic powder

1. Mix rutabaga with garlic powder and avocado oil and put it in the air fryer.
2. Cook the rutabaga bites at 360F for 20 minutes. Shake them from time to time to avoid burning.

The Super Easy Air Fryer Cookbook

Vegetable Roast

Prep time: 5 minutes | Cook time: 20 minutes | Serves 4

- 1 cup cauliflower, chopped
- 6 oz asparagus, chopped
- 1 tablespoon coconut oil
- 1 teaspoon Italian seasonings
- 1 teaspoon salt

1. Put all ingredients in the air fryer basket and shake well.
2. Cook the vegetables at 380F for 20 minutes. Stir them after 10 minutes of cooking.

Radishes

Prep time: 15 minutes | Cook time: 10 minutes | Serves 4

- 1/8 teaspoon pepper
- ½ tablespoon minced fresh oregano
- 1/4 pounds radishes, trimmed and quartered
- 1/8 teaspoon salt
- 2 tablespoons olive oil

1. To make the radishes, preheat your air fryer to 375°F.
2. Toss the radishes with all other ingredients until coated. Grease the tray, put the radishes on it, and cook until crisp-tender, about 12-15 minutes, stirring occasionally.

Baked Bell Peppers Salad

Prep time: 5 minutes | Cook time: 10 minutes | Serves 4

- 1 cup bell pepper, chopped
- 1 teaspoon avocado oil
- 1 teaspoon olive oil
- 1 teaspoon dried cilantro
- ½ cup Mozzarella, shredded

1. Mix bell pepper with avocado oil and put it in the air fryer.
2. Cook the vegetables for 10 minutes at 385F. Shake the bell peppers from time to time.
3. Then mix cooked bell peppers with olive oil, cilantro, and Mozzarella. Shake the cooked salad.

Kidney Bean Popcorn

Prep time: 5 minutes | Cook time: 25 minutes | Serves 2

- 1can kidney beans
- olive oil cooking spray
- 1 teaspoon sea salt

1. To make Air-fried kidney beans, preheat an air fryer to 325 °F (165 °C).
2. Then use olive oil to spray kidney beans and toss with sea salt.
3. Spread them out in a single layer in the air fryer basket, then air-fry until you see that all kidney beans have split open and become crispy, 25 to 30 minutes.
4. If they look under-toasted, fry for another 5 minutes; they would have varying degrees of brown.
5. Now let it cool down for a while and store in an airtight container.

56 | *The Super Easy Air Fryer Cookbook*

Acorn Squash Slices

Prep time: 15 minutes | Cook time: 15 minutes | Serves 6

- ½ cup butter
- 2 acorn squash
- 2/3 cup brown sugar

1. Preheat the air fryer to 350°F.
2. Cut squash in half lengthwise, remove and discard the seeds, and then cut each half crosswise into half-inch slices.
3. Arrange the squash on a greased tray in the air fryer basket; cook until tender, about 5 minutes per side.
4. Meanwhile, combine sugar and butter; spread over the squash and cook for 3 minutes longer.

Air Fryer Sweet Potato

Prep time: 5 minutes | Cook time: 8 minutes | Serves 2

- 1 sweet potato
- Pinch of kosher salt and freshly ground black pepper
- 1 tsp olive oil

1. Cut the peeled sweet potato in French fries. Coat with salt, pepper, and oil.
2. Cook in the air fryer for 8 minutes, at 400 degrees. Cook potatoes in batches, in single layers.
3. Shake once or twice. Serve with your favorite sauce.

Air Fryer Avocado Fries

Prep time: 10 minutes | Cook time: 10 minutes | Serves 2

- 1 avocado
- 1 egg
- 1/2 cup whole wheat bread crumbs
- 1/2 teaspoon salt

1. Cut the avocado into wedges.
2. In a bowl, beat egg with salt. In another bowl, add the bread crumbs.
3. Coat wedges in egg, then in crumbs.
4. Air fry them at 400°F for 8-10 minutes. Toss halfway through.

Chapter 7

Vegan & Vegetarian

Elegant Garlic Mushroom

Prep time: 10 minutes | Cook time: 20 minutes |Serves 3

- 2 tbsp vermouth
- 1/2 tsp garlic powder
- 1 tbsp olive oil
- 2 tsp herbs
- 1 tbsp duck fat

1. Preheat your air fryer to 350 F, add duck fat, garlic powder and herbs in a blender, and process.
2. Pour the mixture over the mushrooms and cover with vermouth.
3. Place the mushrooms in the cooking basket and cook for minutes.
4. Top with more vermouth and cook for 5 more minutes.

Cheesy Kale

Prep time: 10 minutes | Cook time: 15 minutes |Serves 2

- 1/2 lb. kale
- 8 oz. parmesan cheese, shredded
- 1 onion, diced
- 1 tsp. butter
- 1 cup heavy cream

1. Dice up the kale, discarding any hard stems.
2. Get a small baking dish enough to fit inside the fryer, combine the kale with the parmesan, onion, butter, and cream.
3. Pre-heat the fryer at 390°F.
4. Set the baking dish in the fryer and cook for twelve minutes. Make sure to give it a good stir before serving.

Nutmeg Okra

Prep time: 10 minutes |Cook time: 10 minutes |Serves 4

- 1-pound okra, trimmed
- 3 oz pancetta, sliced
- ½ teaspoon ground nutmeg
- ½ teaspoon salt
- 1 teaspoon sunflower oil

1. Sprinkle okra with ground nutmeg and salt.
2. Then put the vegetables in the air fryer and sprinkle with sunflower. Chop pancetta roughly.
3. Top the okra with pancetta and cook the meal for 10 minutes at 360F.

Kid-Friendly Zucchini Fries

Prep time: 10 minutes | Cook time: 20 minutes | Serves 4

- 2 tablespoons olive oil
- 1/2 teaspoon smoked cayenne pepper
- 1 large zucchini, peeled and cut into 1/4-inch long slices
- 1/2 teaspoon shallot powder
- 1/3 teaspoon freshly ground black pepper, or more to taste
- 3/4 teaspoon garlic salt

1. Firstly, preheat your Air Fryer to 360 degrees F.
2. Then, add the zucchini to a mixing dish; toss them with the other ingredients.
3. Cook the zucchini fries approximately 14 minutes. Serve with a dipping sauce of choice.

Paprika Asparagus

Prep time: 5 minutes |Cook time: 10 minutes |Serves 4

- 1 pound asparagus, trimmed
- 3 tablespoons olive oil
- a pinch of salt and black pepper
- 1 tablespoon sweet paprika

1. In a bowl, mix the asparagus with the rest of the ingredients and toss.
2. Put the asparagus in your air fryer's basket and cook at 400 degrees F for 10 minutes.
3. Divide between plates and serve.

Vegetable Salsa Wraps

Prep time: 10 minutes | Cook time: 15 minutes | Serves 4

- 1 cup red onion, sliced
- 1 zucchini, chopped
- 1 poblano pepper, deveined and finely chopped
- 1 head lettuce
- 1/2 cup salsa (homemade or store-bought)
- 8 ounces mozzarella cheese

1. Begin by preheating your Air Fryer to 390 degrees F.
2. Cook red onion, zucchini, and poblano pepper until they are tender and fragrant or about 7 minutes.
3. Divide the sautéed mixture among lettuce leaves; spoon the salsa over the top. Finish off with mozzarella cheese. Wrap lettuce leaves around the filling. Enjoy!

The Super Easy Air Fryer Cookbook

Sriracha Golden Cauliflower

Prep time: 5 minutes | Cook time: 17 minutes | Serves 4

- 1/4 cup vegan butter, melted
- 1/4 cup sriracha sauce
- 4 cups cauliflower florets
- 1 cup breadcrumbs
- 1 teaspoon salt

1. Preheat the air fryer oven to 375F (191C).
2. Mix the sriracha and vegan butter in a bowl and pour this mixture over the cauliflower, taking care to cover each floret entirely.
3. Get another bowl. Mix the breadcrumbs and salt.
4. Dip the cauliflower florets in the breadcrumbs, coating each one well. Put them in the air fryer basket and set time to 17 minutes. Serve hot.

Paprika Kale and Olives

Prep time: 5 minutes | Cook time: 15 minutes | Serves 4

- 1 an ½ pounds kale, torn
- 2 tablespoons olive oil
- salt and black pepper to the taste
- 1 tablespoon hot paprika
- 2 tablespoons black olives, pitted and sliced

1. In a pan that fits the air fryer, combine all the ingredients and toss.
2. Put the pan in your air fryer, cook at 370 degrees F for 15 minutes, divide between plates and serve.

Crispy Black-Eyed Peas

Prep time: 10 minutes | Cook time: 10 minutes | Serves 6

- 15-ounces black-eyed peas
- 1/8 teaspoon chipotle chili powder
- ¼ teaspoon salt
- ½ teaspoon chili powder
- 1/8 teaspoon black pepper

1. Rinse the beans well with running water then set aside. In a large bowl, mix the spices until well combined. Add the peas to spices and mix.
2. Place the peas in the wire basket and cook for 10-minutes at 360°Fahrenheit. Serve and enjoy!

The Super Easy Air Fryer Cookbook

Caribbean Fried Peppers With Tofu

Prep time: 10 minutes | Cook time: 20 minutes | Serves 2

- 2 bell peppers, peeled and cut into slices
- 6 ounces firm tofu, cut into cubes
- 2 tablespoons avocado oil
- 2 teaspoons Caribbean Sorrel Rum Spice Mix

1. Toss the bell peppers and tofu with the avocado oil and spice mix.
2. Cook in the preheated Air Fryer at 400 degrees F for 10 minutes, shaking the cooking basket halfway through the cooking time.
3. Adjust the seasonings to taste and enjoy!

Spicy Celery Sticks

Prep time: 10 minutes | Cook time: 20 minutes | Serves 4

- 1 pound celery, cut into matchsticks
- 2 tablespoons peanut oil
- 1 jalapeño, seeded and minced
- 1/4 teaspoon dill
- 1/2 teaspoon basil
- Salt and white pepper to taste

1. Start by preheating your Air Fryer to 380 degrees F.
2. Toss all ingredients together and place them in the Air Fryer basket.
3. Cook for 15 minutes, shaking the basket halfway through the cooking time. Transfer to a serving platter and enjoy!

Lemony Green Beans

Prep time: 10 minutes | Cook time: 12 minutes | Serves 3

- 1-pound green beans, trimmed and halved
- 1 teaspoon butter, melted
- 1 tablespoon fresh lemon juice
- 1/4 teaspoon garlic powder

1. Preheat the Air fryer to 400 o F and grease an Air fryer basket.
2. Mix all the ingredients in a bowl and toss to coat well.
3. Arrange the green beans into the Air fryer basket and cook for about 12 minutes.
4. Dish out in a serving plate and serve hot.

Balsamic Garlic Kale

Prep time: 2 minutes |Cook time: 12 minutes |Serves 6

- 2 tablespoons olive oil
- 3 garlic cloves, minced
- 2 and ½ pounds kale leaves
- salt and black pepper to the taste
- 2 tablespoons balsamic vinegar

1. In a pan that fits the air fryer, combine all the ingredients and toss.
2. Put the pan in your air fryer and cook at 300 degrees F for 12 minutes.
3. Divide between plates and serve.

Zucchini Balls

Prep time: 5 minutes | Cook time:10 minutes |Serves 4

- 4 zucchinis
- 1 egg
- 1/2 cup grated Parmesan cheese
- 1 tablespoon Italian herbs
- 1 cup grated coconut

1. Thinly grate the zucchinis and dry with a cheesecloth, ensuring to remove all the moisture.
2. Blend and mix well zucchinis with the egg, Parmesan, Italian herbs, and grated coconut in a bowl.
3. Form the mixture into balls.
4. Preheat the air fryer oven to 400F (204C).
5. Lay the zucchini balls in the air fryer basket and cook for 10 minutes.
6. Serve hot.

Tangy Asparagus And Broccoli

Prep time: 10 minutes | Cook time: 25 minutes | Serves 4

- 1/2 pound asparagus, cut into 1 1/2-inch pieces
- 1/2 pound broccoli, cut into 1 1/2-inch pieces
- 2 tablespoons peanut oil
- Some salt and white pepper, to taste
- 1/2 cup chicken broth
- 2 tablespoons apple cider vinegar

1. Place the vegetables in a single layer in the lightly greased cooking basket. Drizzle the peanut oil over the vegetables.
2. Sprinkle with salt and white pepper.
3. Cook at 380 degrees F for 15 minutes, shaking the basket halfway through the cooking time.
4. Add 1/2 cup of chicken broth to a saucepan; bring to a rapid boil and add the vinegar. Cook for 5 to 7 minutes or until the sauce has reduced by half.
5. Spoon the sauce over the warm vegetables and serve immediately. Bon appétit!

Sesame Fennel

Prep time: 10 minutes |Cook time: 15 minutes |Serves 2

- 8 oz fennel bulb
- 1 teaspoon sesame oil
- ½ teaspoon salt
- 1 teaspoon white pepper

1. Trim the fennel bulb and cut it into halves.
2. Then sprinkle the fennel bulb with salt, white pepper, and sesame oil.
3. Preheat the air fryer to 370F.
4. Put the fennel bulb halves in the air fryer and cook them for 15 minutes.

Potato with Creamy Cheese

Prep time: 5 minutes | Cook time:15 minutes |Serves 2

- 2 medium potatoes
- 1 teaspoon butter
- 3 tablespoons sour cream
- 1 teaspoon chives
- 1 1/2 tablespoons grated Parmesan cheese

1. Preheat the air fryer oven to 350 degrees F.
2. Stick the potatoes with a fork and boil them in water until they are cooked. Move to the air fryer basket and cook for 15 minutes.
3. In the meantime, combine the sour cream, cheese, and chives in bowl.
4. Cut the potatoes halfway to open them up and fill with the butter and sour cream mixture.
5. Serve immediately.

Crispy Brussels Sprout Chips

Prep time: 10 minutes | Cook time: 20 minutes | Serves 2

- 10 Brussels sprouts, separated into leaves
- 1 teaspoon canola oil
- 1 teaspoon coarse sea salt
- 1 teaspoon paprika

1. Toss all ingredients in the lightly greased Air Fryer basket.
2. Bake at 380 degrees F for 15 minutes, shaking the basket halfway through the cooking time to ensure even cooking.
3. Serve and enjoy!

Coconut Mushrooms Mix

Prep time: 5 minutes |Cook time: 15 minutes |Serves 4

- 1 pound brown mushrooms, sliced
- 1 pound kale, torn
- Salt and black pepper to the taste
- 2 tablespoons olive oil
- 14 ounces coconut milk

1. In a pan that fits your air fryer, mix the kale with the rest of the ingredients and toss.
2. Put the pan in the fryer, cook at 380 degrees F for 15 minutes, divide between plates and serve.

Chili Lime Broccoli

Prep time: 5 minutes |Cook time: 15 minutes |Serves 4

- 1 pound broccoli florets
- 2 tablespoons olive oil
- 2 tablespoons chili sauce
- juice of 1 lime
- a pinch of salt and black pepper

1. In a bowl, mix the broccoli with the other ingredients and toss well.
2. Put the broccoli in your air fryer's basket and cook at 400 degrees F for 15 minutes.
3. Divide between plates and serve.

Garden Fresh Green Beans

Prep time: 10 minutes | Cook time:12 minutes |Serves 4

- 1-pound green beans, washed and trimmed
- 1 teaspoon butter, melted
- 1 tablespoon fresh lemon juice
- 1/4 teaspoon garlic powder
- Salt and freshly ground pepper, to taste

1. Preheat the Air fryer to 400 F and grease an Air fryer basket.
2. Put all the ingredients in a large bowl and transfer into the Air fryer basket.
3. Cook for about 8 minutes and dish out in a bowl to serve warm.

Chapter 8

Desserts

Blackberry Cream

Prep time: 4 minutes |Cook time: 20 minutes |Serves 6

- 2 cups blackberries
- juice of ½ lemon
- 2 tablespoons water
- 1 teaspoon vanilla extract
- 2 tablespoons swerve

1. In a bowl, mix all the ingredients and whisk well.
2. Divide this into 6 ramekins, put them in the air fryer and cook at 340 degrees F for 20 minutes Cool down and serve.

Deep Fried Snickers

Prep time: 10 minutes | Cook time: 6 minutes | Serves 10

- 10 fun size snickers bars
- 8 oz crescent rolls tube
- 1 tablespoon butter, melted

1. To make chocolate-dipped snickers, remove crescent rolls from the tube, unroll dough, and place on baking sheet.
2. Cut out 10 squares; wrap each one with a piece of dough. Pinch seams and cuts well to seal completely.
3. Brush dough with melted butter and place on baking sheet.
4. Air Fry at 370°F for 6 minutes or until golden brown. Top with powdered sugar, whipped cream, and drizzle on chocolate sauce.

Cocoa Spread

Prep time: 10 minutes |Cook time: 5 minutes |Serves 4

- 2 oz walnuts, chopped
- 5 teaspoons coconut oil
- ½ teaspoon vanilla extract
- 1 tablespoon erythritol
- 1 teaspoon of cocoa powder

1. Preheat the air fryer to 350F. Put the walnuts in the mason jar.
2. Add coconut oil, vanilla extract, Erythritol, and cocoa powder. Stir the mixture until smooth with the help of the spoon.
3. Then place the mason jar with Nutella in the preheated air fryer and cook it for 5 minutes. Stir Nutella before serving.

The Super Easy Air Fryer Cookbook

Keto Butter Balls

Prep time: 15 minutes | Cook time: 10 minutes | Serves 4

- 1 tablespoon butter, softened 1 tablespoon erythritol
- ½ teaspoon ground cinnamon
- 1 tablespoon coconut flour
- 1 teaspoon coconut flakes
- cooking spray

1. Put the butter, Erythritol, ground cinnamon, coconut flour, and coconut flakes.
2. Then stir the mixture with the help of the fork until homogenous.
3. Make 4 balls. Preheat the air fryer to 375F. Spray the air fryer basket with cooking spray and place the balls inside. Cook the dessert for 10 minutes.

Baked Molten Lava Cake

Prep time: 5 minutes | Cook time: 10 minutes | Serves 4

- 1.5 tablespoon self-rising flour
- 3.5 tablespoon baker's sugar
- 3.5 oz unsalted butter
- 3.5 oz dark chocolate
- 2 eggs

1. Grease and flour four standard oven-safe ramekins. Melt chocolate and butter in a bowl that is microwave safe for about 3 minutes, stir it continuously so that chocolate and butter are well combined.
2. Whisk/beat the eggs and sugar until pale and frothy. Pour melted chocolate mixture into egg mixture. Stir in flour, using a spatula to combine everything evenly.
3. Pour the cake mixture into ramekins, and bake in a preheated air fryer at 375°F for 10 minutes. Remove from the air fryer, let cool for 2 minutes inside each ramekin (or just 1 minute if using silicone ones), then turn upside down onto serving plate or platter (tapping the bottom of each ramekin with a butter knife to loosen edges if necessary).
4. Cake should release from ramekin with little effort, and the center should appear dark/gooey once served warm a la mode or drizzled with raspberry sauce.

Almond Cookies

Prep time: 5 minutes |Cook time: 15 minutes |Serves 8

- 1 and ½ cups almonds, crushed
- 2 tablespoons erythritol
- ½ teaspoon baking powder
- ¼ teaspoon almond extract
- 2 eggs, whisked

1. In a bowl, mix all the ingredients and whisk well.
2. Scoop 8 servings of this mix on a baking sheet that fits the air fryer which you've lined with parchment paper.
3. Put the baking sheet in your air fryer and cook at 350 degrees F for 15 minutes. Serve cold.

Pineapple Sticks with Yogurt Dip

Prep time: 10 minutes | Cook time: 10 minutes | Serves 2

- ¼ cup dried coconut
- ½ pineapple

Yogurt Dip:
- 1 cup vanilla yogurt
- 1 sprig of fresh mint

1. Preheat your air fryer to 390°Fahrenheit. Cut the pineapple into sticks. Dip pineapple sticks into the dried coconut.
2. Place the sticks covered with desiccated coconut into air fryer basket and cook for 10-minutes. Prepare the yogurt dip. Dice the mint leaves and combine with vanilla yogurt and stir. Serve pineapple sticks with yogurt dip and enjoy!

Spiced Apples

Prep time: 5 minutes | Cook time:17 minutes |Serves 4

- 4 small apples, cored, sliced
- 2 tablespoons erythritol sweeteners
- 1 teaspoon apple pie spice
- 2 tablespoons olive oil

1. Switch on the air fryer, insert fryer basket, grease it with olive oil, then shut with its lid, set the fryer at 350 degrees F, and preheat for 5 minutes.
2. Meanwhile, place apple slices in a bowl, sprinkle with sweetener and spice, and drizzle with oil and stir until evenly coated.
3. Open the fryer, add apple slices in it, close with its lid and cook for 12 minutes until nicely golden and crispy, shaking halfway through the frying.
4. Serve straight away.

The Super Easy Air Fryer Cookbook

Italian Cheese Chips

Prep time: 10 minutes | Cook time: 15 minutes | Serves 4

- 1 cup Parmesan cheese, shredded
- 1 cup Cheddar cheese, shredded
- 1 teaspoon Italian seasoning
- 1/2 cup marinara sauce

1. Start by preheating your Air Fryer to 350 degrees F. Place a piece of parchment paper in the cooking basket.
2. Mix the cheese with the Italian seasoning.
3. Add about 1 tablespoon of the cheese mixture (per crisp) to the basket, making sure they are not touching. Bake for 6 minutes or until browned to your liking.
4. Work in batches and place them on a large tray to cool slightly. Serve with the marinara sauce. Bon appétit!

Almond Bars

Prep time: 5 minutes |Cook time: 12 minutes |Serves 12

- 1 teaspoon vanilla extract
- 1 cup almond butter, soft
- 1 egg
- 2 tablespoons erythritol

1. In a bowl, mix all the ingredients and whisk really well.
2. Spread this on a baking sheet that fits the air fryer lined with parchment paper, introduce in the fryer and cook at 350 degrees F and bake for 12 minutes.
3. Cool down, cut into bars and serve.

Cream Cups

Prep time: 5 minutes |Cook time: 10 minutes |Serves 6

- 2 tablespoons butter, melted
- 8 ounces cream cheese, soft
- 3 tablespoons coconut, shredded and unsweetened
- 3 eggs
- 4 tablespoons swerve

1. In a bowl, mix all the ingredients and whisk really well.
2. Divide into small ramekins, put them in the fryer and cook at 320 degrees F and bake for 10 minutes.
3. Serve cold.

Lemon Berry Jam

Prep time: 10 minutes |Cook time: 20 minutes |Serves 12

- ¼ cup swerve
- 8 ounces strawberries, sliced
- 1 tablespoon lemon juice
- ¼ cup water

1. In a pan that fits the air fryer, combine all the ingredients, put the pan in the machine and cook at 380 degrees F for 20 minutes.
2. Divide the mix into cups, cool down and serve.

Peanut Cookies

Prep time: 15 minutes |Cook time: 5 minutes |Serves 4

- 4 tablespoons peanut butter
- 4 teaspoons erythritol
- 1 egg, beaten
- ¼ teaspoon vanilla extract

1. In the mixing bowl mix up peanut butter, Erythritol, egg, and vanilla extract.
2. Stir the mixture with the help of the fork. Then make 4 cookies. Preheat the air fryer to 355F.
3. Place the cookies in the air fryer and cook them for 5 minutes.

Chocolate Bacon Bites

Prep time: 5 minutes |Cook time: 10 minutes |Serves 4

- 4 bacon slices, halved
- 1 cup dark chocolate, melted
- a pinch of pink salt

1. Dip each bacon slice in some chocolate, sprinkle pink salt over them, put them in your air fryer's basket and cook at 350 degrees F for 10 minutes.
2. Serve as a snack.

Apple Hand Pies

Prep time: 10 minutes | Cook time:10 minutes |Serves 6

- 15-ounces no-sugar-added apple pie filling
- 1 store-bought crust

1. Layout pie crust and slice into equal-sized squares.
2. Place 2 tbsp. Filling into each square and seal crust with a fork.
3. Place into the fryer. Cook 8 minutes at 390 degrees until golden in color.

The Super Easy Air Fryer Cookbook

Berry Cookies

Prep time: 15 minutes |Cook time: 9 minutes |Serves 4

- 2 teaspoons butter, softened
- 1 tablespoon splenda
- 1 egg yolk
- ½ cup almond flour
- 1 oz strawberry, chopped, mashed

1. In the mixing bowl mix up butter, Splenda, egg yolk, and almond flour. Knead the non-sticky dough. Then make the small balls from the dough.
2. Use your finger to make small holes in every ball. Then fill the balls with mashed strawberries. Preheat the air fryer to 360F.
3. Line the air fryer basket with baking paper and put the cookies inside. Cook them for 9 minutes.

Chocolate Hazelnut Turnovers

Prep time: 10 minutes | Cook time: 10 minutes | Serves 12

- 1 frozen puff pastry sheet
- 3 tablespoons chopped hazelnuts
- powdered sugar
- ⅓ cup chocolate-hazelnut spread
- 1 egg

1. To make the turnovers, preheat the air fryer to 400°F. Line a baking sheet with parchment paper and lightly flour it. Make sure you have an extra-large bowl of ice water nearby.
2. Place one sheet of puff pastry on a floured surface, then roll it out until it is 9 x 12 inches in size. With a sharp knife cut each piece into 3 x 3-inch squares. In one of the centers of each square, place about 1 teaspoon chocolate hazelnut spread and sprinkle with hazelnuts.
3. Fold each triangle in half diagonally so that it forms a triangle that looks like a diamond. Brush the edges of each triangle with egg mixture and press together to seal them in place.
4. Arrange these triangles on their baking sheet and repeat until all pieces are done.

Midnight Nutella Banana Sandwich

Prep time: 5 minutes | Cook time: 8 minutes | Serves 2

- 4 slices of bread
- ¼ cup chocolate hazelnut spread
- 1 banana

1. First, preheat the air fryer to 370°F. Spread softened butter on half of one bread slice, then place the other bread slice, buttered side down on top.
2. Spread chocolate hazelnut spread on the other half of bread slice, and then place a banana half on each piece of bread.
3. Cut each half into three pieces lengthwise and place them on two slices of bread with remaining bread slices making two sandwiches.
4. Cut in half(triangle or rectangle)to fit in air fryer at once. Transfer sandwiches to a hot ring and fry for 5 minutes until browned.
5. Flip over sandwiches and fry for another 2 to 3 minutes or until desired crispiness is reached. Pour yourself a glass of milk or nightcap while waiting for sandwiches to cool slightly. Enjoy!!

Cinnamon Sugar Dessert Fries

Prep time: 5 minutes | Cook time: 15 minutes | Serves 4

- 2 sweet potatoes
- 1 tablespoon butter
- 1/2 teaspoon cinnamon
- 2 tablespoons sugar

1. Preheat your air fryer to 380°F. Peel and cut the sweet potatoes into thin fries.
2. Coat the fries with 1 tablespoon of butter, then cook them in the preheated air fryer for 15-18 minutes. They should not fill your air fryer more than 1/2 full and should overlap one another so they do not burn on the outside before they are cooked through on the inside.
3. When they are done cooking, remove them and place them into a bowl with 1 teaspoon of butter and 1 teaspoon of brown sugar, then mix well. They are ready to eat immediately!

Apple Dumplings

Prep time: 10 minutes | Cook time:25 minutes |Serves 4

- 2 tbsp. melted coconut oil
- 2 puff pastry sheets
- 1 tbsp. brown sugar
- 2 tbsp. raisins
- 2 small apples of choice

1. Ensure your air fryer is preheated to 356 degrees F.
2. Core and peel apples and mix with raisins and sugar.
3. Place a bit of apple mixture into puff pastry sheets and brush sides with melted coconut oil.
4. Place into air fryer. Cook 25 minutes, turning halfway through. It will be golden when done.

Appendix 1 Measurement Conversion Chart

Volume Equivalents (Dry)

US STANDARD	METRIC (APPROXIMATE)
1/8 teaspoon	0.5 mL
1/4 teaspoon	1 mL
1/2 teaspoon	2 mL
3/4 teaspoon	4 mL
1 teaspoon	5 mL
1 tablespoon	15 mL
1/4 cup	59 mL
1/2 cup	118 mL
3/4 cup	177 mL
1 cup	235 mL
2 cups	475 mL
3 cups	700 mL
4 cups	1 L

Volume Equivalents (Liquid)

US STANDARD	US STANDARD (OUNCES)	METRIC (APPROXIMATE)
2 tablespoons	1 fl.oz.	30 mL
1/4 cup	2 fl.oz.	60 mL
1/2 cup	4 fl.oz.	120 mL
1 cup	8 fl.oz.	240 mL
1 1/2 cup	12 fl.oz.	355 mL
2 cups or 1 pint	16 fl.oz.	475 mL
4 cups or 1 quart	32 fl.oz.	1 L
1 gallon	128 fl.oz.	4 L

Temperatures Equivalents

FAHRENHEIT(F)	CELSIUS(C) APPROXIMATE)
225 °F	107 °C
250 °F	120 ° °C
275 °F	135 °C
300 °F	150 °C
325 °F	160 °C
350 °F	180 °C
375 °F	190 °C
400 °F	205 °C
425 °F	220 °C
450 °F	235 °C
475 °F	245 °C
500 °F	260 °C

Weight Equivalents

US STANDARD	METRIC (APPROXIMATE)
1 ounce	28 g
2 ounces	57 g
5 ounces	142 g
10 ounces	284 g
15 ounces	425 g
16 ounces (1 pound)	455 g
1.5 pounds	680 g
2 pounds	907 g

Appendix 2 The Dirty Dozen and Clean Fifteen

The Environmental Working Group (EWG) is a nonprofit, nonpartisan organization dedicated to protecting human health and the environment Its mission is to empower people to live healthier lives in a healthier environment. This organization publishes an annual list of the twelve kinds of produce, in sequence, that have the highest amount of pesticide residue-the Dirty Dozen-as well as a list of the fifteen kinds of produce that have the least amount of pesticide residue-the Clean Fifteen.

THE DIRTY DOZEN

The 2016 Dirty Dozen includes the following produce. These are considered among the year's most important produce to buy organic:

Strawberries	Spinach
Apples	Tomatoes
Nectarines	Bell peppers
Peaches	Cherry tomatoes
Celery	Cucumbers
Grapes	Kale/collard greens
Cherries	Hot peppers

The Dirty Dozen list contains two additional items kale/collard greens and hot peppers-because they tend to contain trace levels of highly hazardous pesticides.

THE CLEAN FIFTEEN

The least critical to buy organically are the Clean Fifteen list. The following are on the 2016 list:

Avocados	Papayas
Corn	Kiw
Pineapples	Eggplant
Cabbage	Honeydew
Sweet peas	Grapefruit
Onions	Cantaloupe
Asparagus	Cauliflower
Mangos	

Some of the sweet corn sold in the United States are made from genetically engineered (GE) seedstock. Buy organic varieties of these crops to avoid GE produce.

Appendix 3 Index

A

almond 11, 15, 16, 27, 30, 52, 69, 70, 72
almond flour 11, 27, 30, 52, 72
apple 28, 31, 37, 46, 47, 53, 55, 63, 69, 71, 73
apple cider vinegar 28, 31, 37, 46, 47, 53, 55, 63
avocado 10, 11, 16, 17, 20, 27, 31, 36, 38, 39

B

bacon 11, 12, 19, 20, 23, 29, 32, 35, 38, 40, 44, 71
balsamic vinegar 26, 35, 63
banana 23, 73
basil 27, 34, 39, 50, 55, 62
bell pepper 52, 56
bread 15, 18, 19, 23, 43, 45, 52, 54, 57, 73
broccoli 17, 53, 63, 65
buns 34
butter 15, 18, 19, 20, 21, 23, 36, 43, 57, 59, 61

C

canola oil 9, 64
cauliflower 16, 21, 54, 56, 61
cayenne 12, 36, 43, 48, 60
cayenne pepper 12, 36, 43, 48
Cheddar cheese 9, 10, 15, 17, 20, 21, 43, 52, 53, 70
cheese 9, 10, 11, 12, 13, 15, 16, 17, 19, 20
chicken 18, 25, 26, 27, 28, 30, 31, 32

chili powder 12, 34, 44, 61
chives 9, 18, 20, 23, 64
chocolate 67, 68, 71, 72, 73
cinnamon 15, 22, 25, 28, 68, 73
coconut 13, 17, 18, 21, 28, 30, 31, 32, 34, 39, 40
coriander 27, 28, 38, 50, 53
corn 9
cumin 12, 50

D

dark chocolate 68, 71
Dijon mustard 26, 34, 55

E

egg 9, 13, 15, 16, 18, 19, 21, 37, 42, 43, 44
erythritol 67, 68, 69, 70, 71

F

flour 11, 27, 30, 52, 68, 72
fresh chives 9
fresh mint 69
fresh parsley 12, 26, 49, 52

G

garlic 9, 13, 17, 18, 27, 28, 29, 31, 32, 36, 40, 42, 44, 45
garlic powder 17, 27, 28, 29, 31, 40, 42

H

hazelnut spread 72, 73
honey 10, 42, 48

J

juice 11, 26, 35, 42, 45, 62, 65, 67, 71

76 | The Super Easy Air Fryer Cookbook

K

kale 59, 61, 63, 64
kale leaves 63
ketchup 10, 34
kosher salt 9, 10, 11, 26, 29, 45, 57

L

lemon 10, 11, 42, 45, 46, 47, 50, 62, 65, 67, 71
lemon juice 11, 42, 62, 65, 71
lime 26, 35, 45, 65
lime juice 35, 45

M

maple syrup 23, 49, 50
marinara sauce 70
milk 16, 21, 64, 73
Mozzarella 10, 27, 52, 54, 56
mushroom 25, 38
mustard 10, 26, 34, 35, 38, 53, 55

N

nutritional yeast 18

O

olive oil 9, 10, 11, 12, 13, 18, 20, 23, 25, 28, 29, 30
onion 11, 25, 28, 35, 38, 47, 52, 53, 59, 60
onion powder 28, 35, 38, 47, 53
oregano 16, 44, 53, 54, 56

P

paprika 12, 13, 18, 20, 21, 23, 25, 26, 29, 31, 38
Parmesan cheese 12, 63, 64, 70
parsley 12, 26, 43, 49, 52, 76
peanut butter 23, 71
potato 52, 57
powder 11, 12, 17, 27, 28, 29, 31
puff pastry 9, 72, 73

R

raisins 73

S

salt 9, 10, 11, 12, 13, 15, 16, 17, 18, 19, 20, 21, 22
sugar 10, 12, 23, 57, 67, 68, 71, 72, 73
syrup 23, 49, 50

T

thyme 9, 32, 38, 39
tomato 11, 13, 18, 27, 31, 36
turmeric 39, 54, 55

U

unsalted butter 20, 68

V

vanilla 67, 69, 70, 71
vegetable broth 13
vinegar 26, 28, 31, 34, 35, 36, 37

W

white wine 13, 27

Y

yogurt 11, 69

Z

zucchini 17, 60, 63

The Super Easy Air Fryer Cookbook | **77**

Deborah J. Ward

Printed in Great Britain
by Amazon